Halloween

Pumpkin

Art

75 Creative Ideas for Halloween Decorating

Written and imagined by Mika Harada

Harajuku Dress to Impress

© 2024 Mika Harada

All rights reserved. Yes, that means you can't photocopy, scan, or share this book in any sneaky way without our permission. While pumpkins love being painted, piracy doesn't look good on anyone—but asking nicely? Always in style!

Disclaimer: No pumpkins were harmed in the making of this book—though a few brushes may have met an untimely splatter. This book is not just pages of pretty pumpkins; it's a celebration of creativity, imagination, and a whole lot of Halloween spirit.

Every image and idea inside was lovingly crafted to inspire you. So grab your paintbrushes, get messy, and let your pumpkins shine! Just remember, if you suddenly find yourself painting pumpkins year-round, we won't judge—we'll cheer you on!

Published by Mika Harada

First Edition

INTRODUCTION

Halloween is one of the most anticipated celebrations of the year, a time where magic, creativity, and mystery come together to create traditions full of excitement and fun. During this season, the streets are filled with costumes, dim lights, and, most of all, decorated pumpkins that capture the spirit of the holiday. But not all pumpkins have to be spooky or dark. In this book, we invite you to explore a wide variety of ideas for painting and decorating pumpkins—from the scariest to the most charming and creative—making sure your pumpkin stands out in a unique way. But there's something unique about the images in this book—they've been brought to life using cutting-edge AI techniques.

The tradition of Halloween pumpkins, known as Jack O'Lanterns, has its roots in an old Irish legend that has endured over centuries. According to the story, a man named Jack, famous for his cunning and tricks, managed to outwit the devil several times, thus avoiding being taken to hell. However, when Jack died, he was not admitted to heaven or hell, so he was condemned to wander the Earth as a lost soul. It is said that Jack carried a hollowed-out turnip with a glowing ember inside to light his way in the dark. Over time, this legend made its way to America, where the turnip was replaced by the pumpkin, which was more plentiful and easier to carve.

Today, carved and decorated pumpkins are an iconic symbol of Halloween. However, the art of decorating pumpkins has evolved. It's no longer just about carving spooky faces; now, painting and other methods of decoration have opened up endless creative possibilities. From elegant and sophisticated designs to fantasy characters and fun figures, painted pumpkins allow everyone—regardless of age—to express their unique vision of Halloween.

In this book, you'll discover inspiring ideas to help you transform an ordinary pumpkin into a masterpiece. Whether you're an experienced artist or it's your first time decorating a pumpkin, there's something here for every skill level. We'll provide helpful tips on what types of paints to use, how to mix colors, and what tools you can employ to add texture and depth to your designs. We've also included some simple techniques that will add a special touch to your creations, making your pumpkins look amazing!

Remember, creativity has no limits. You can choose a traditional pumpkin with a modern twist, like a ghostly face with shiny details, or let your imagination run wild and create a pumpkin inspired by your favorite characters, funny animals, or abstract patterns.

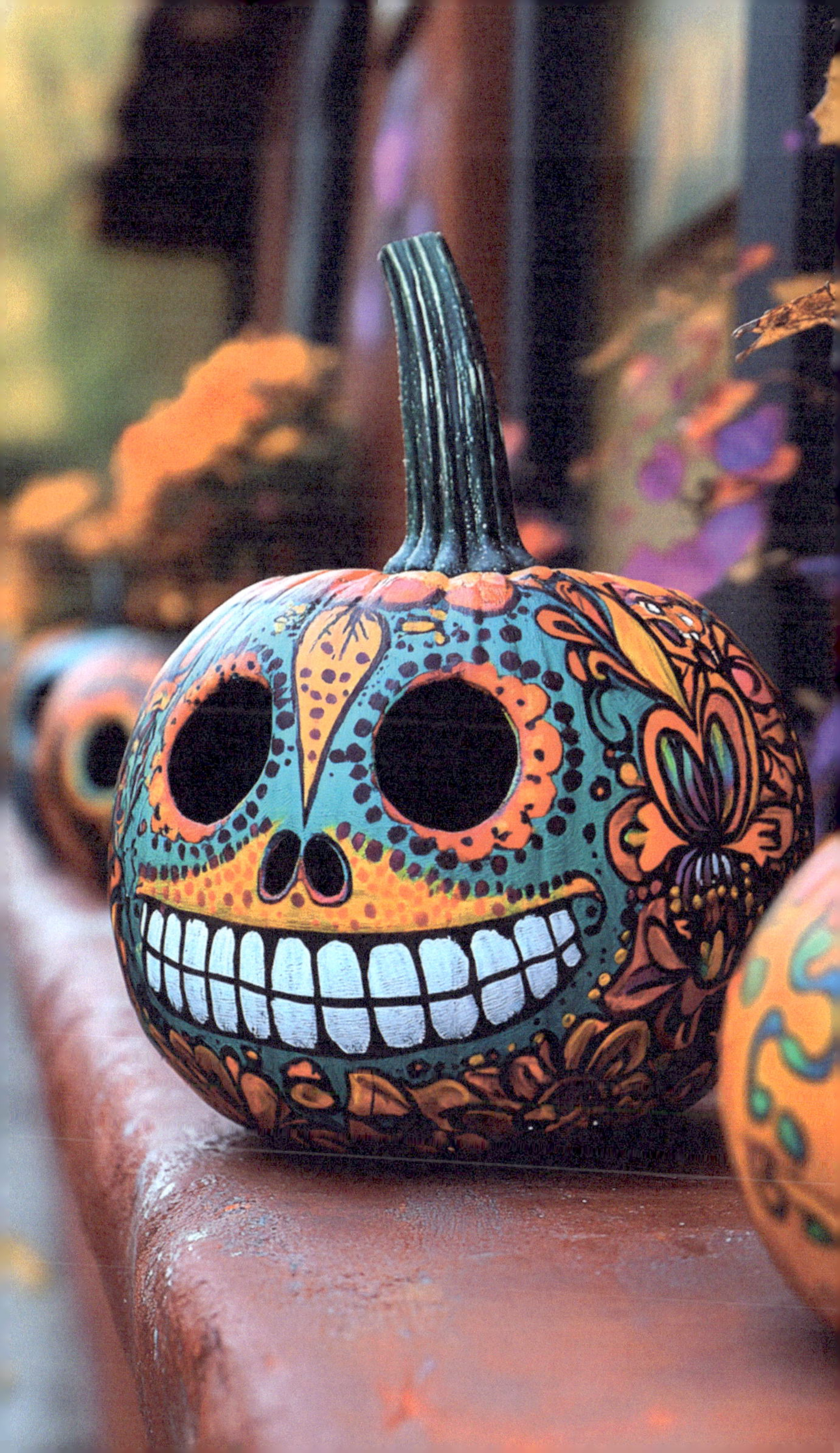

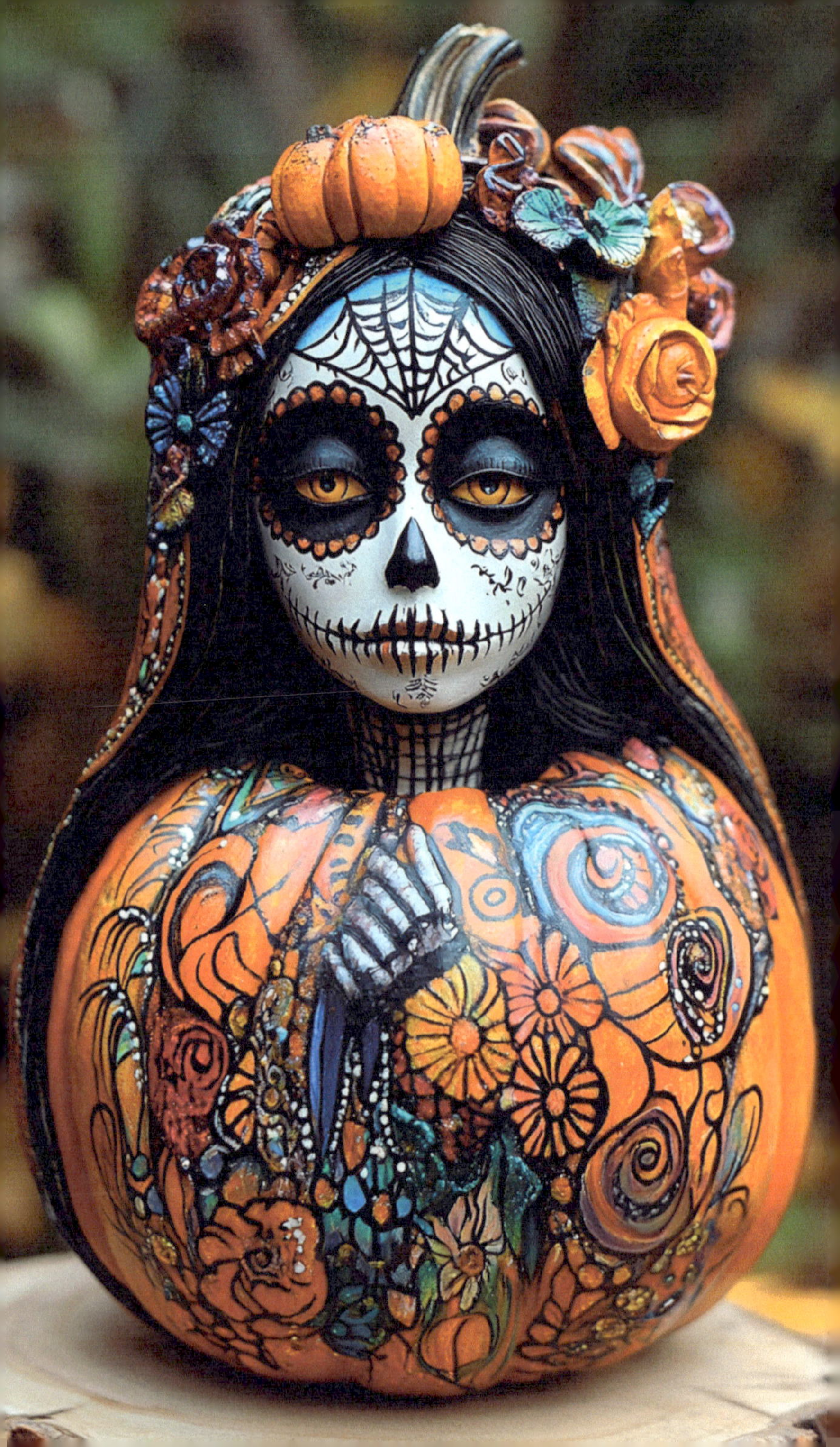

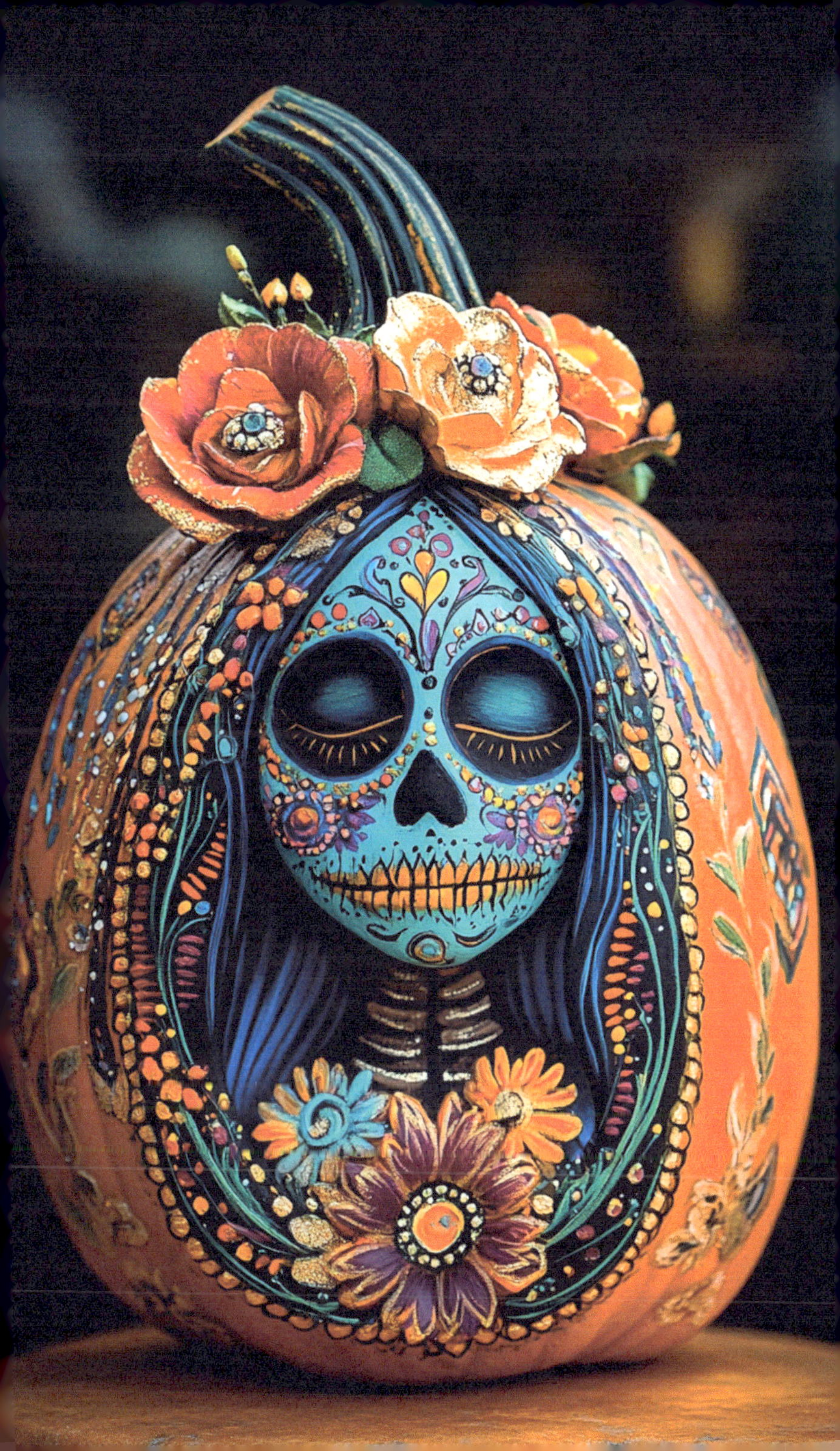

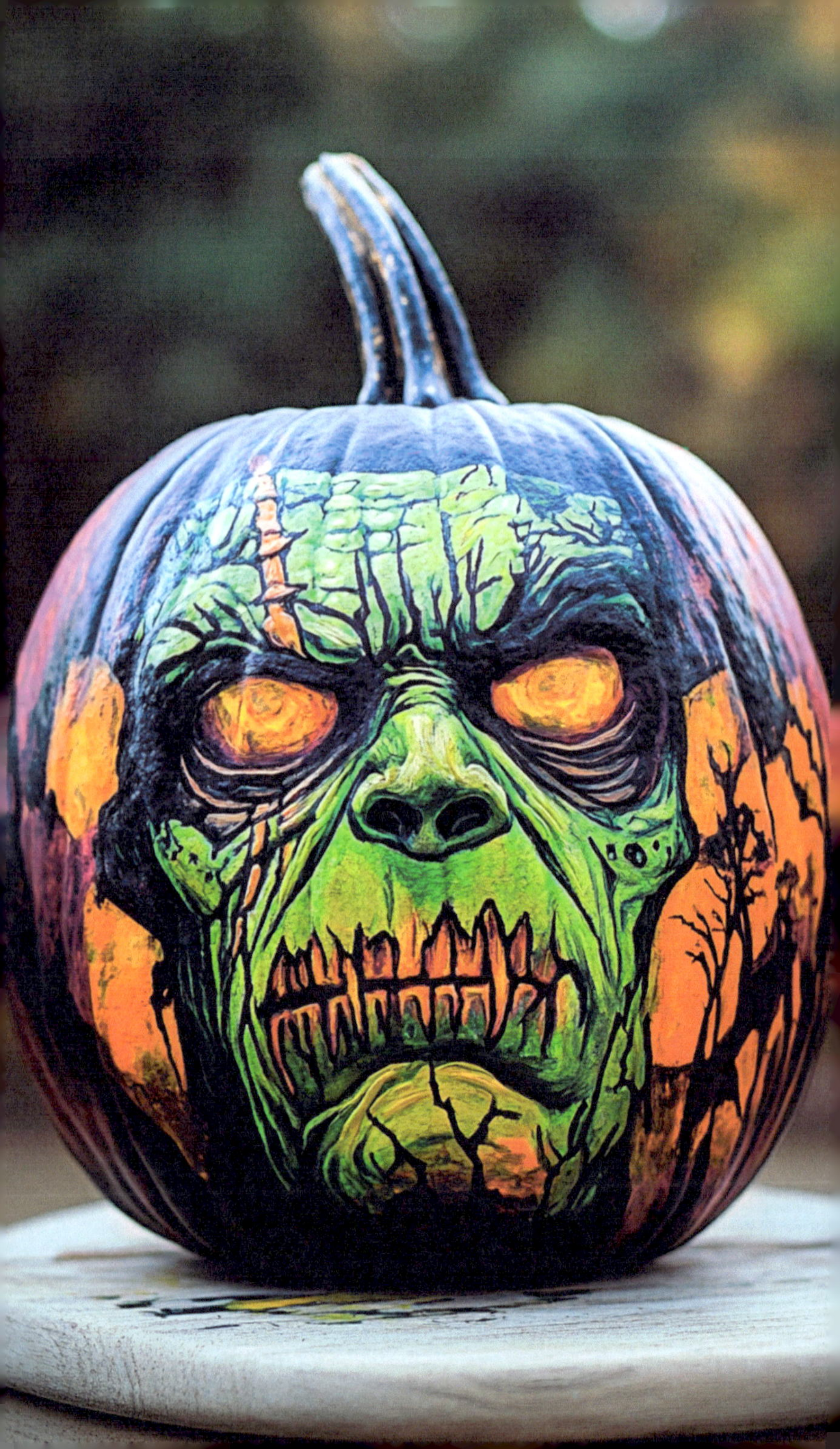

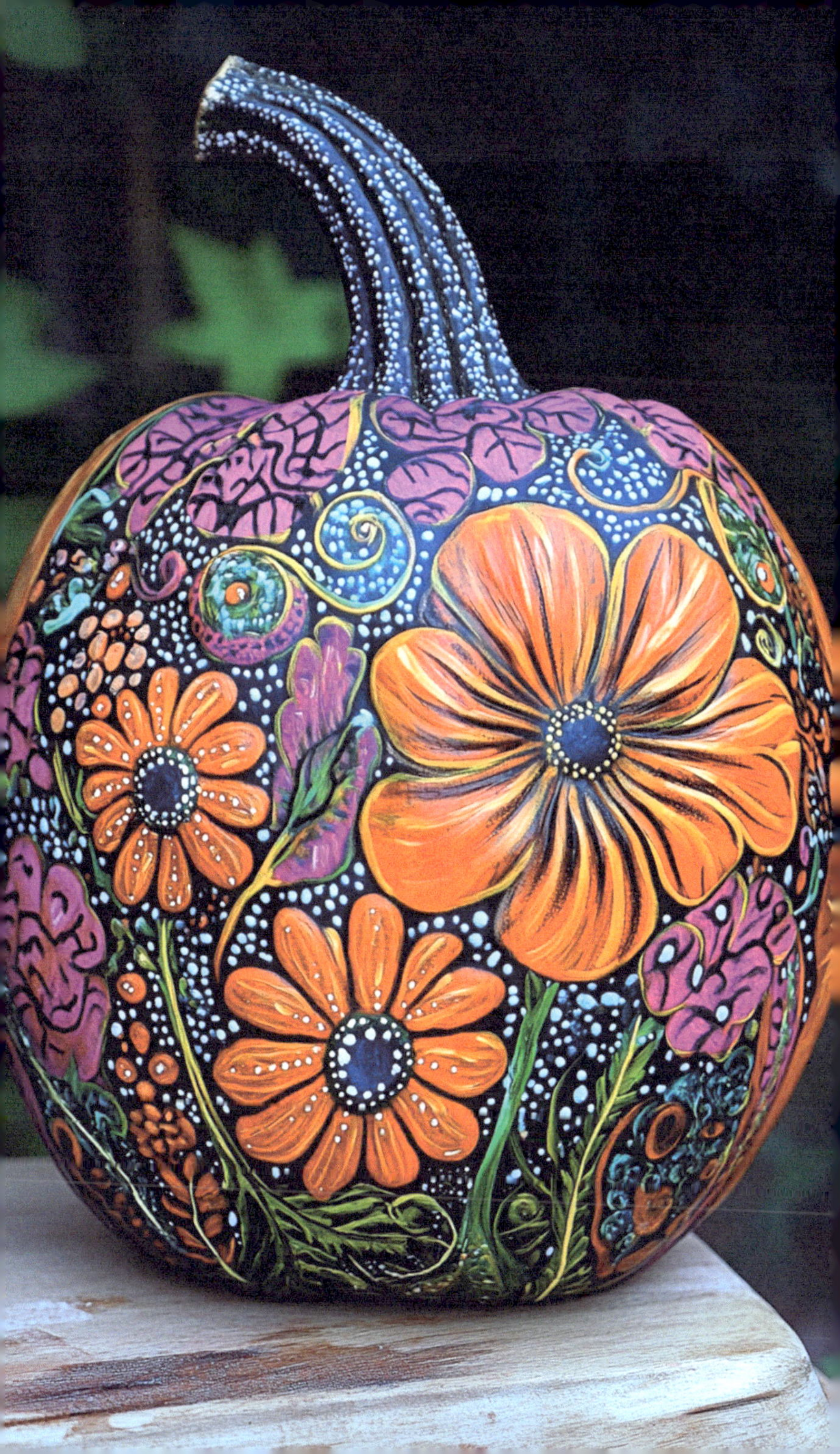

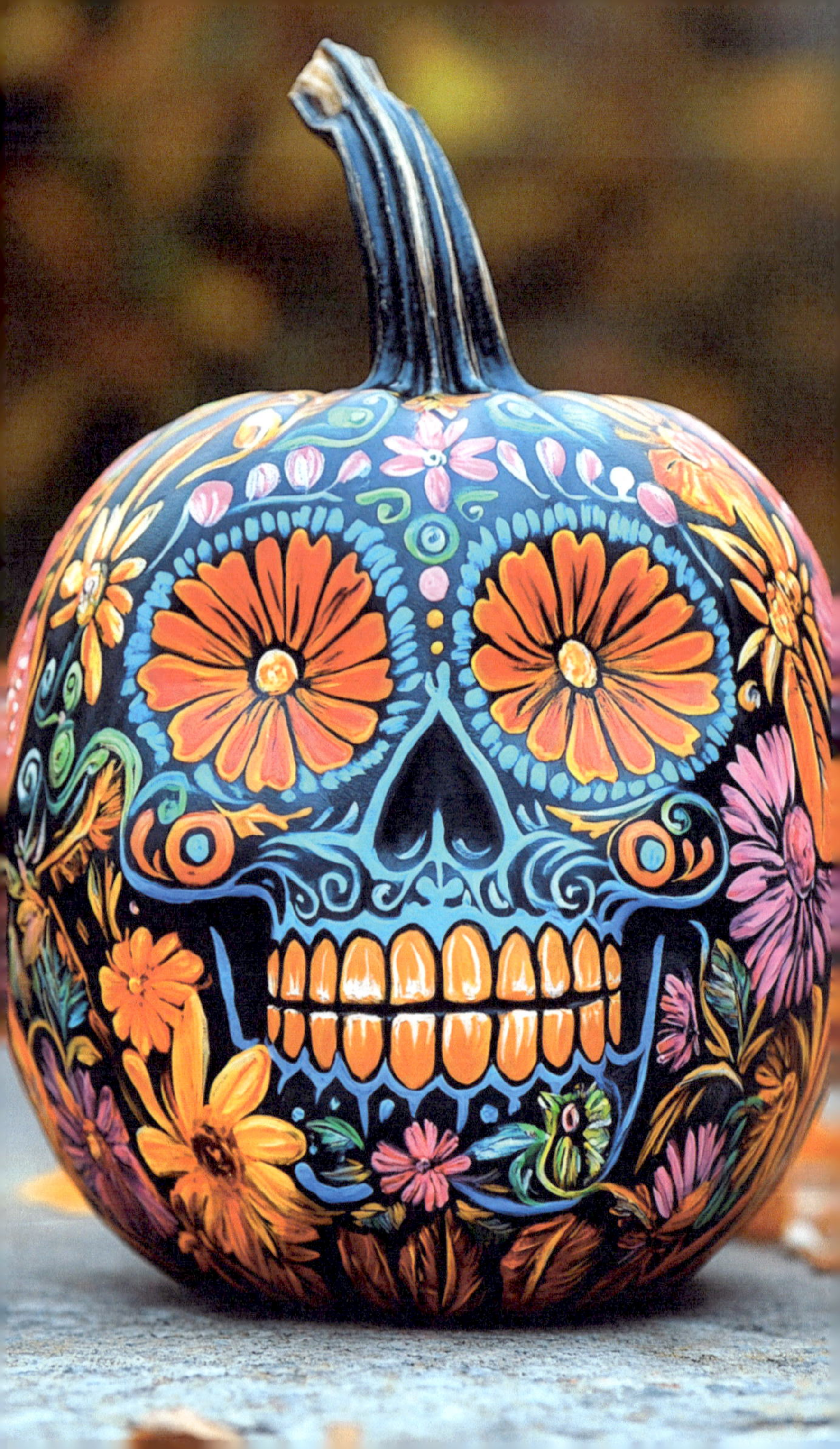

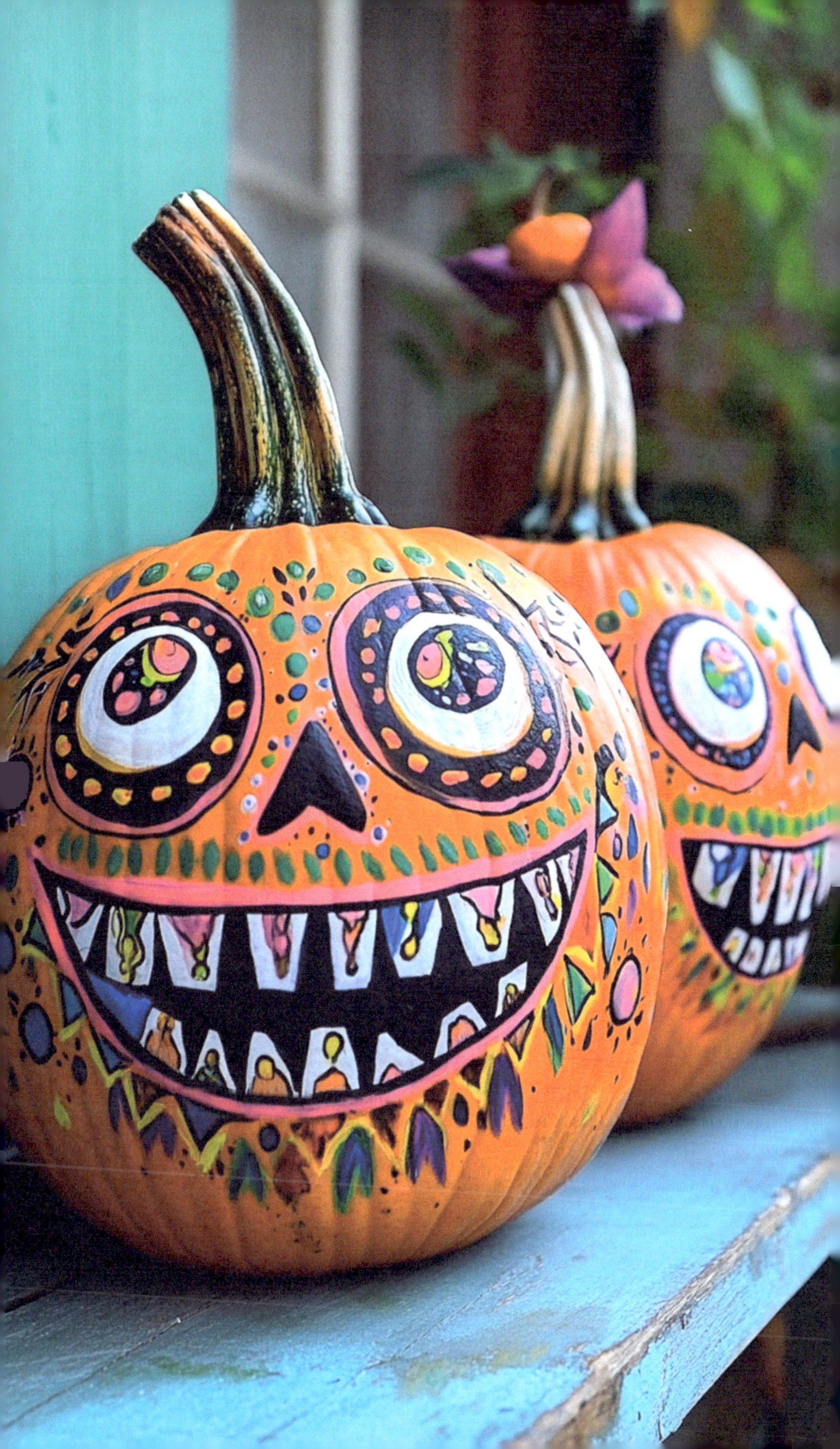

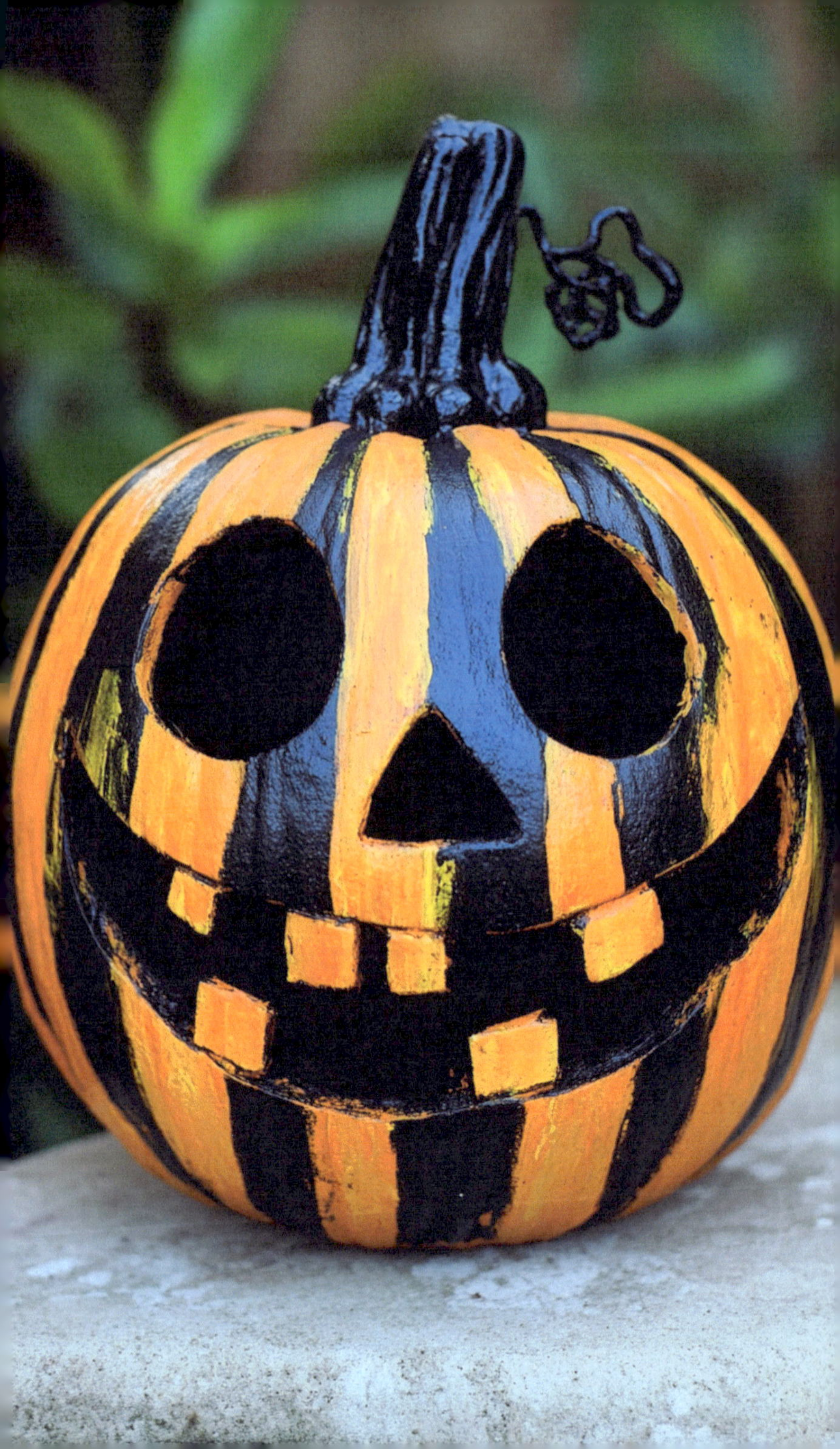

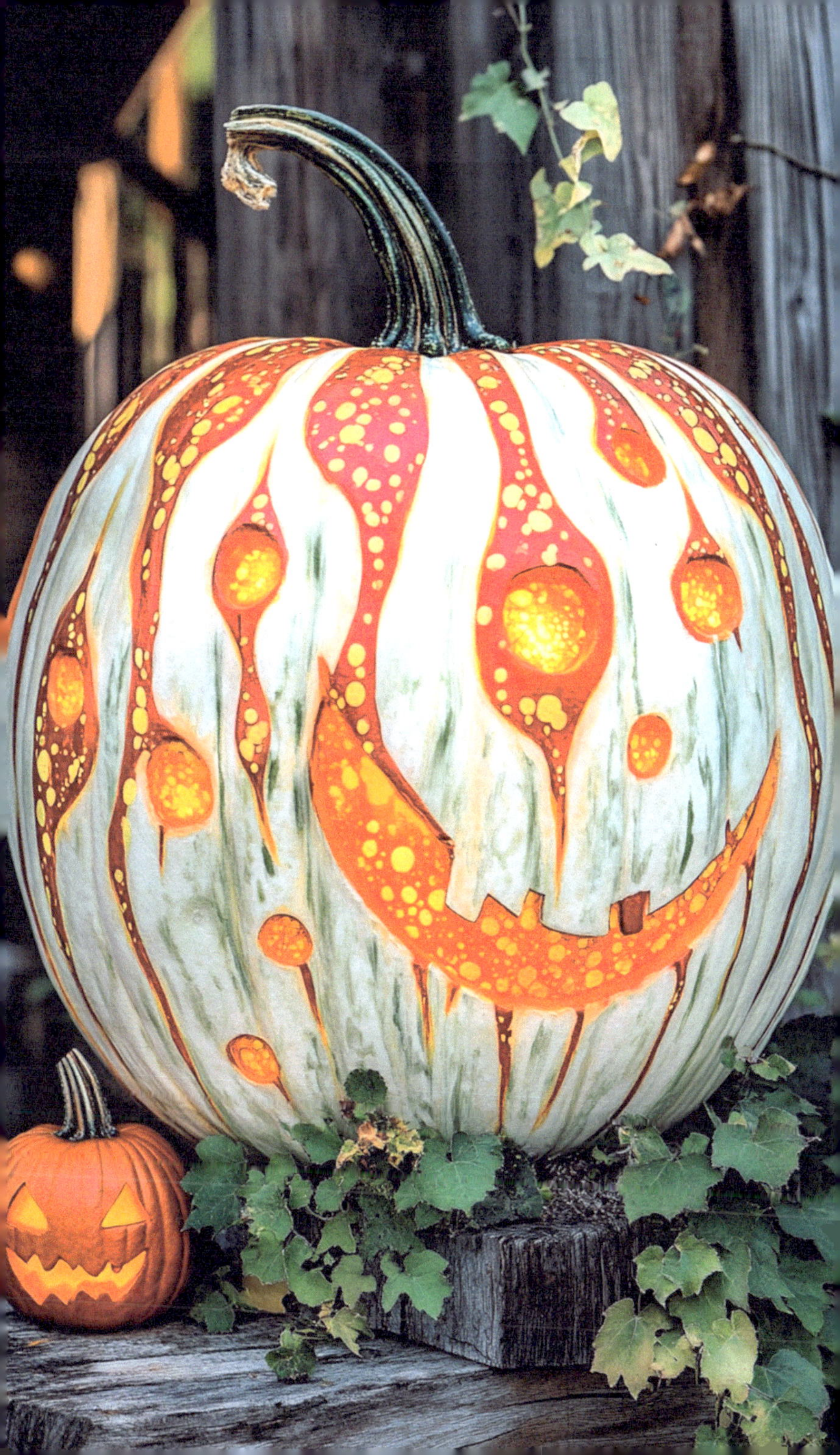

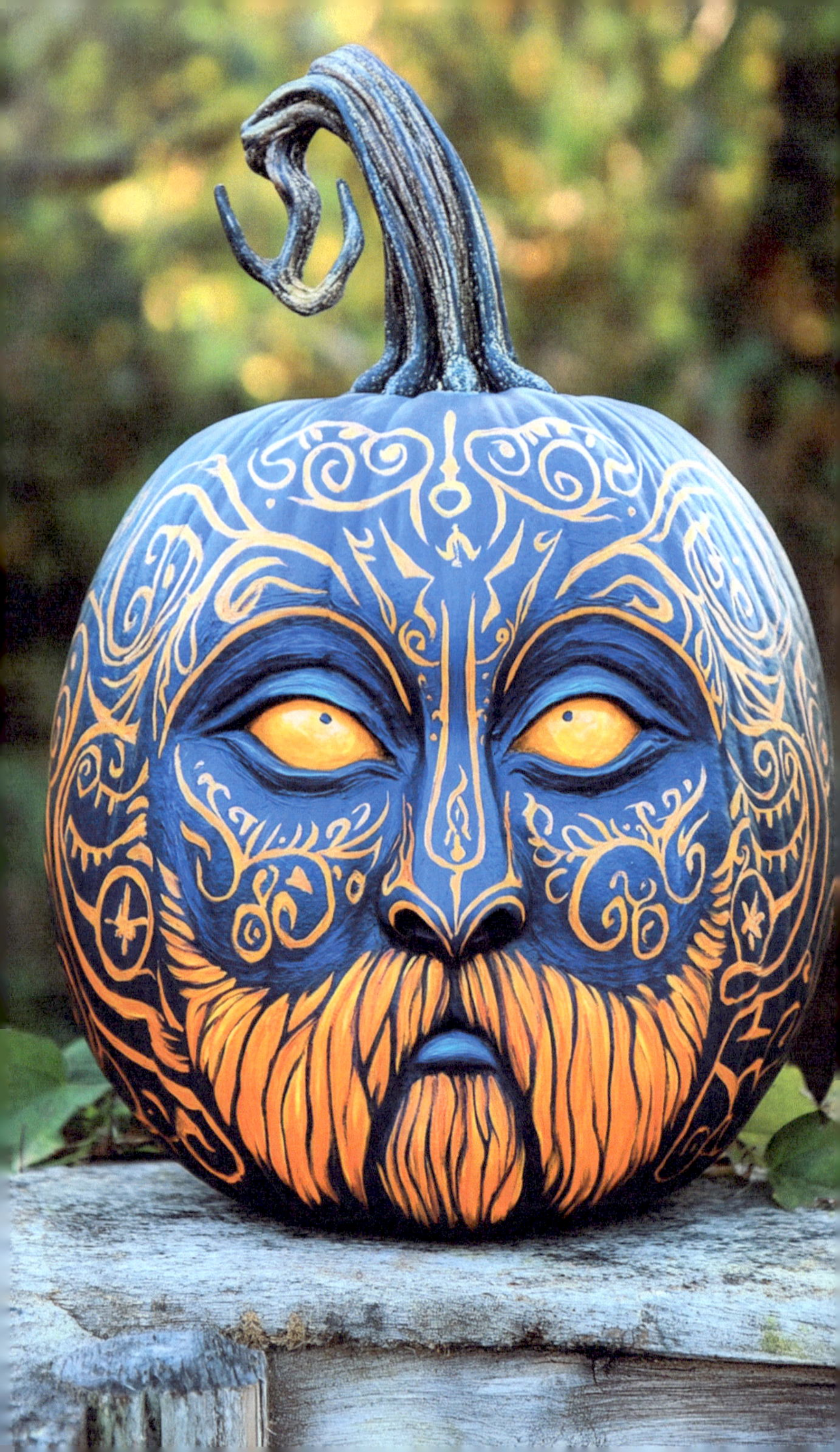

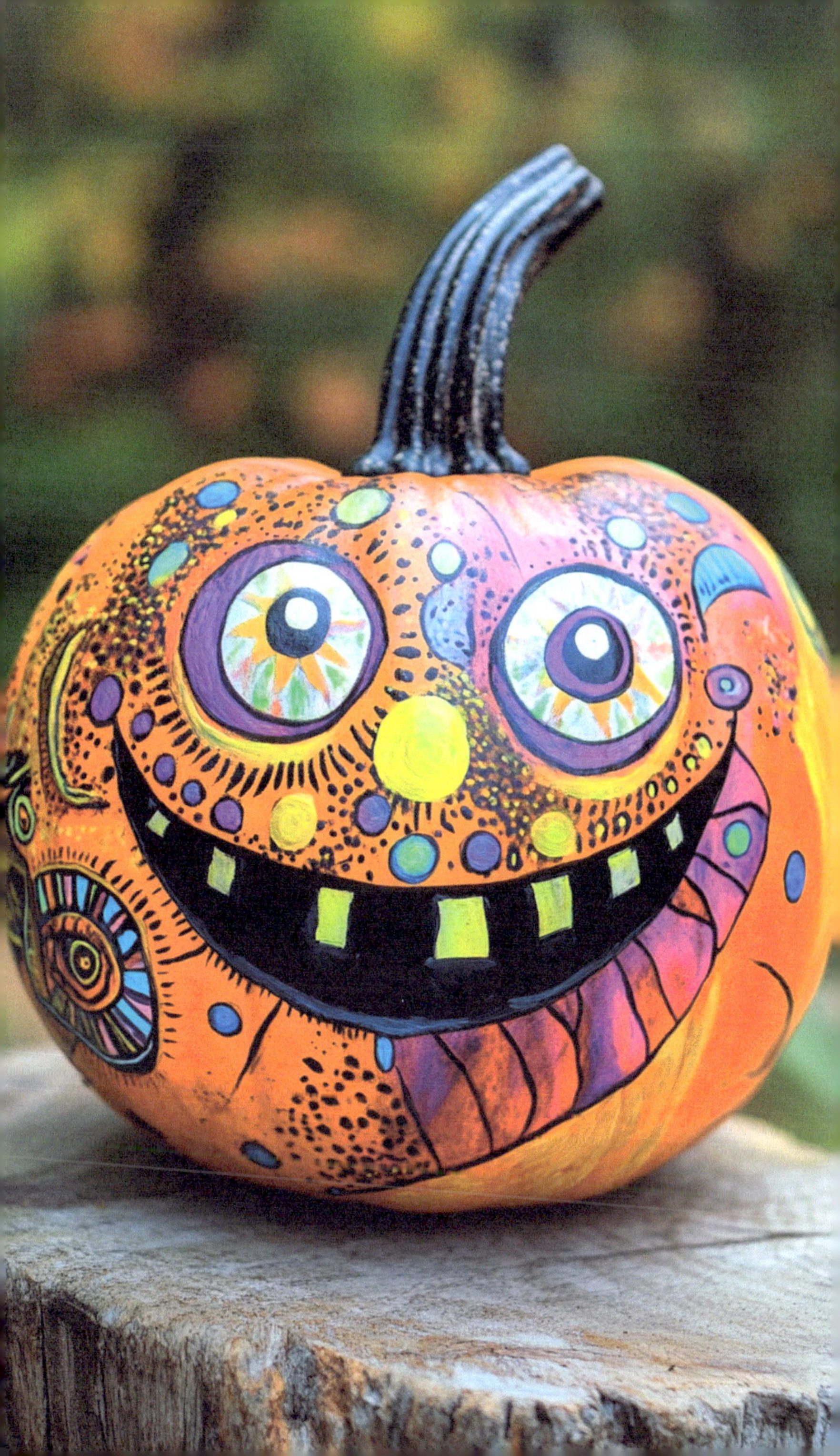

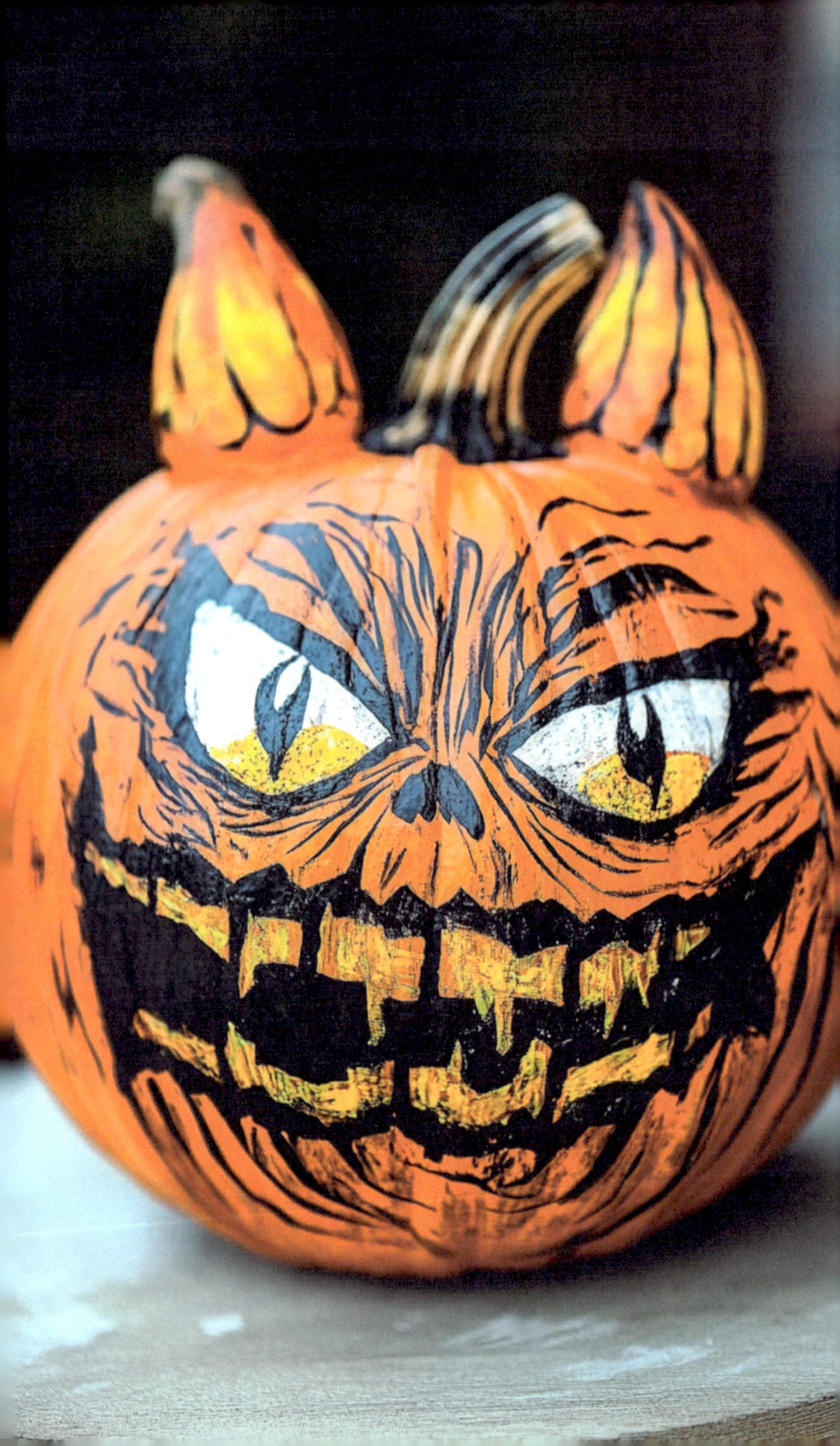

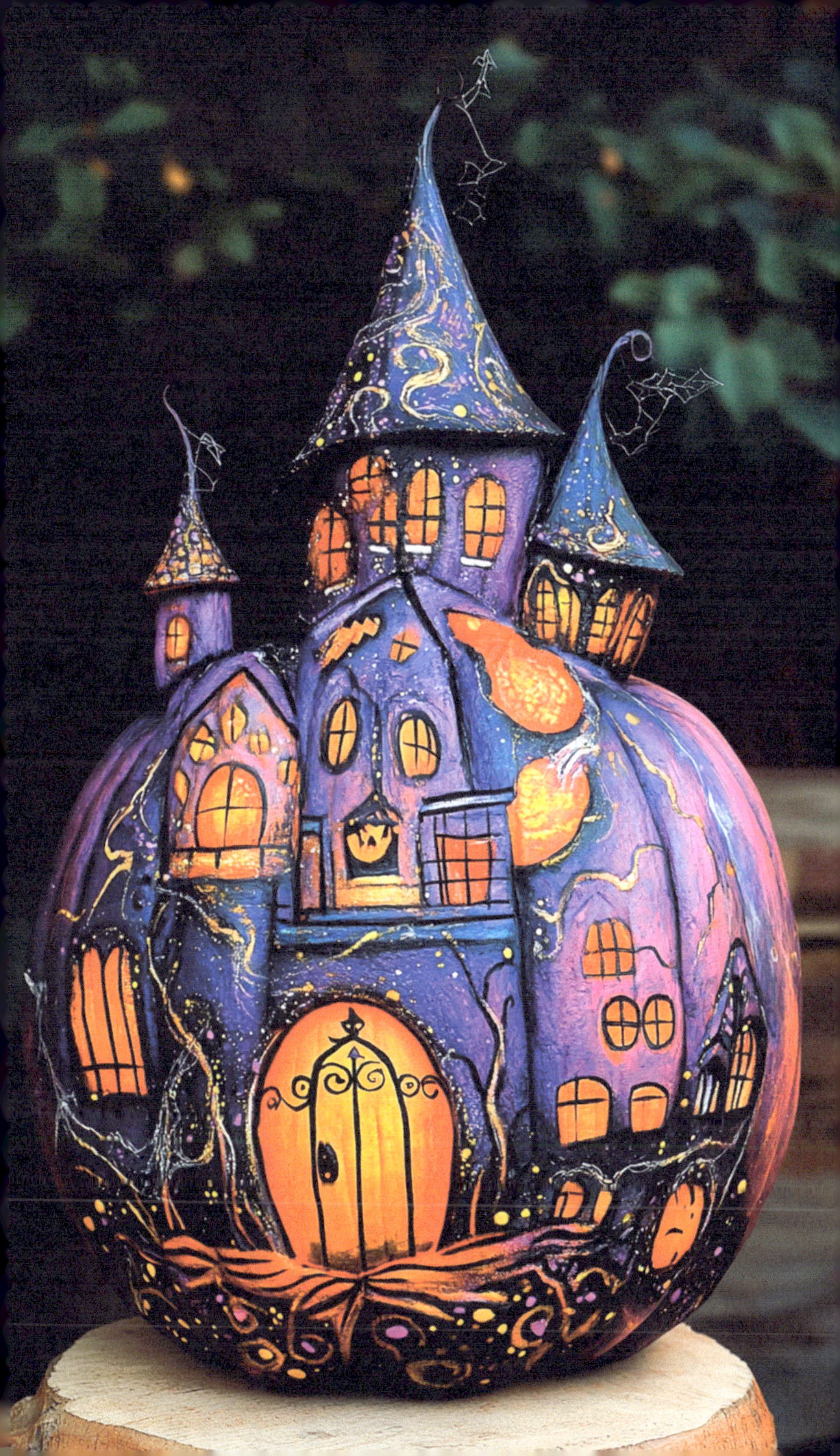

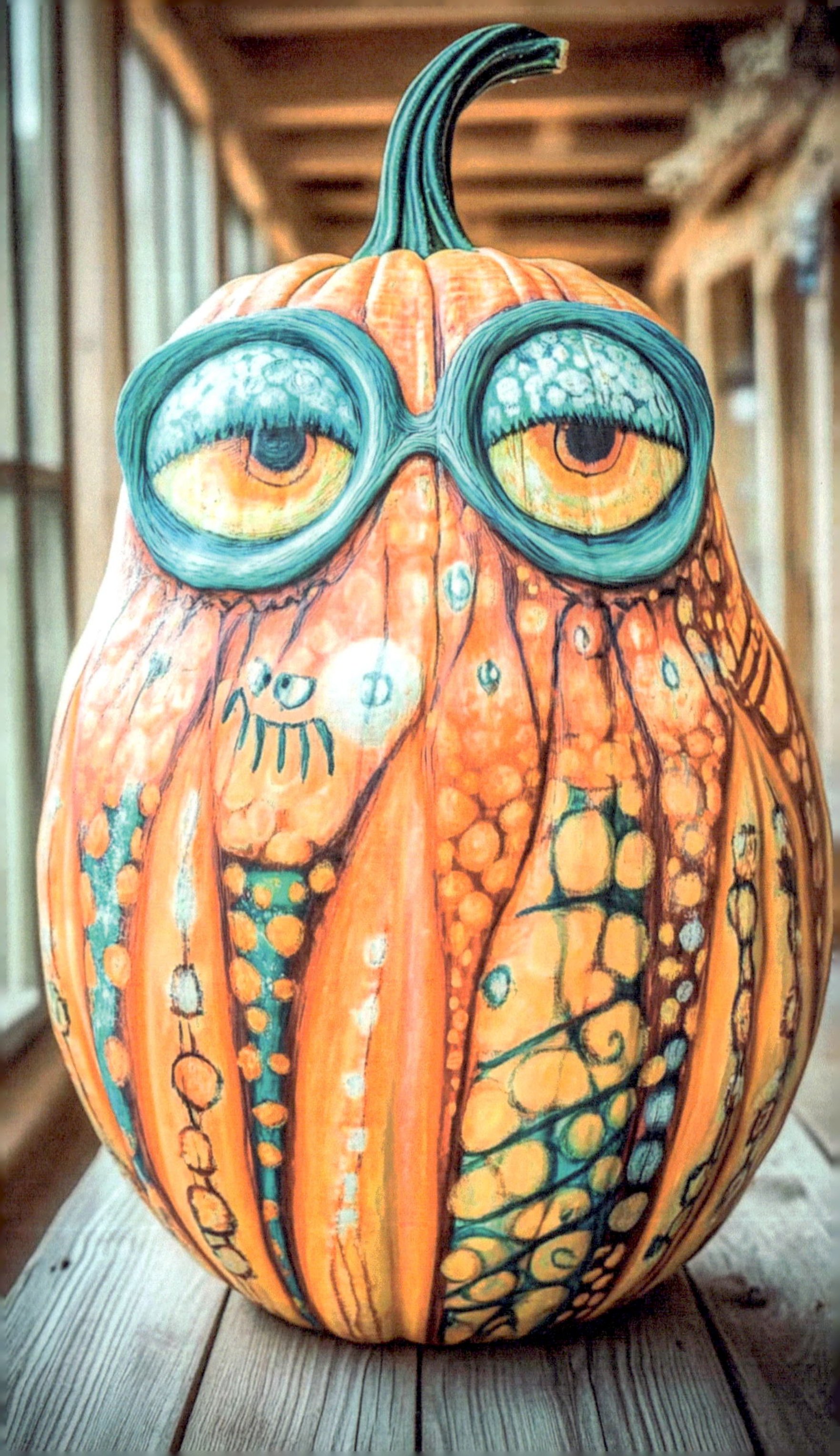

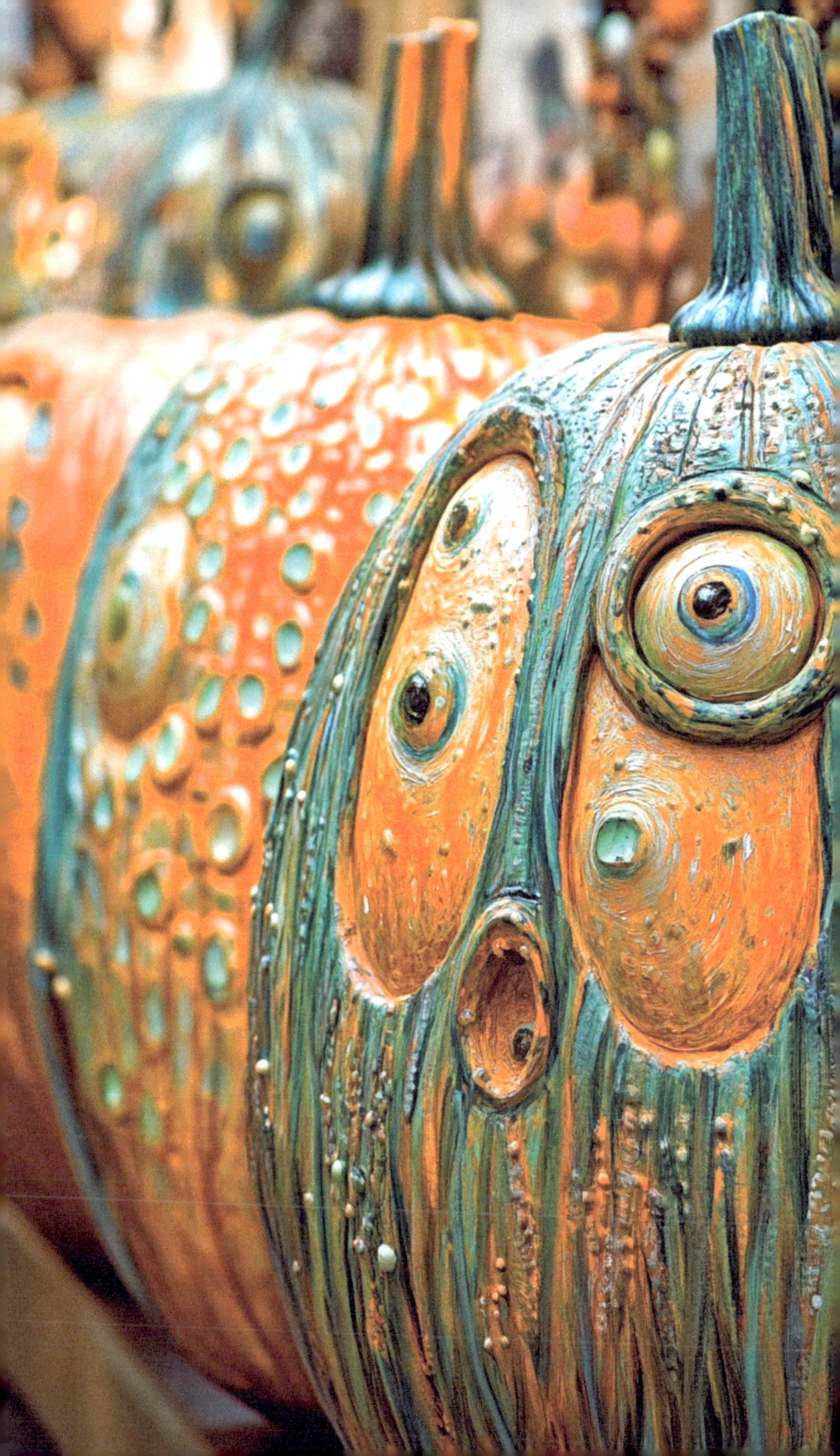

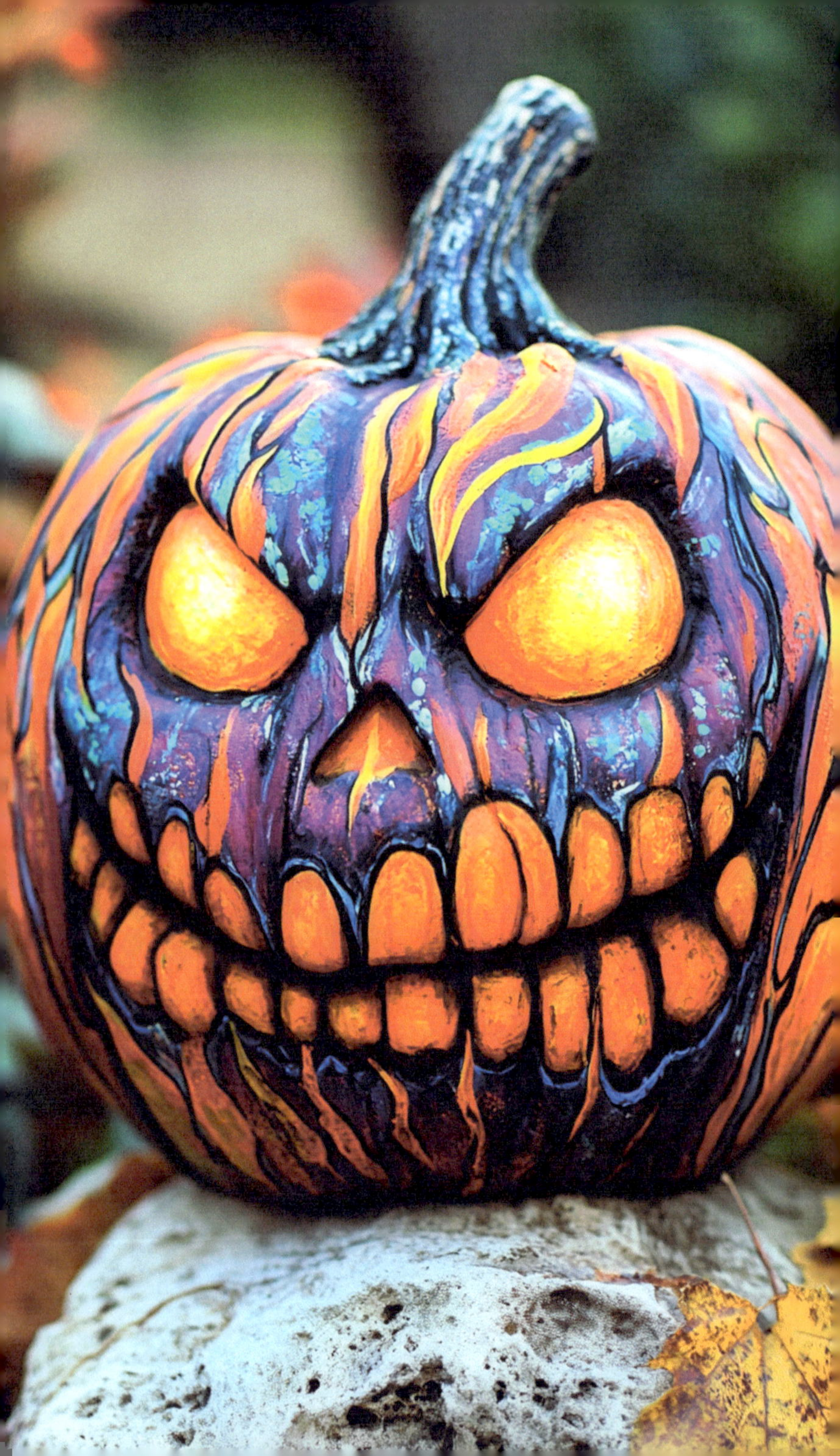

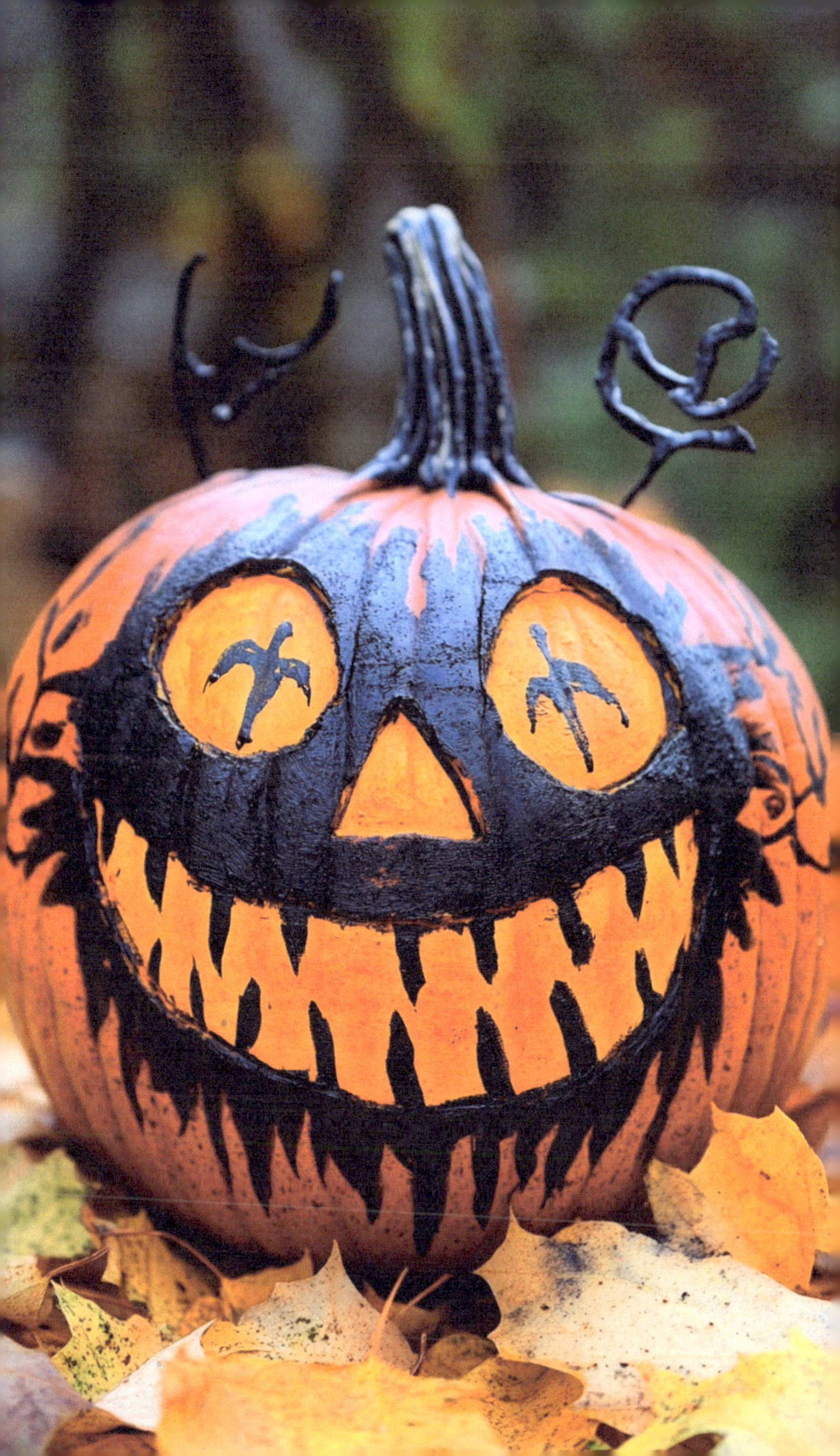

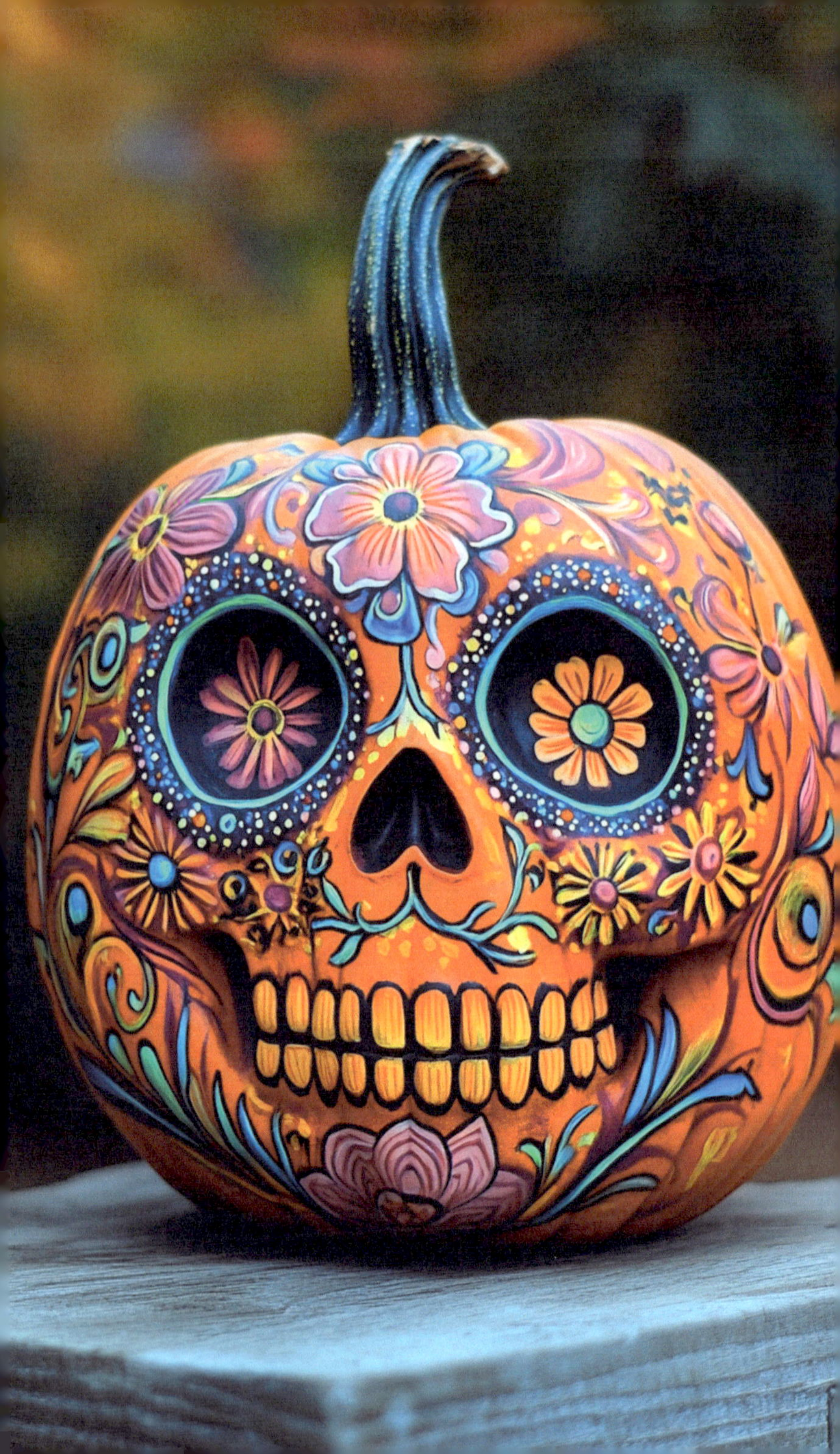

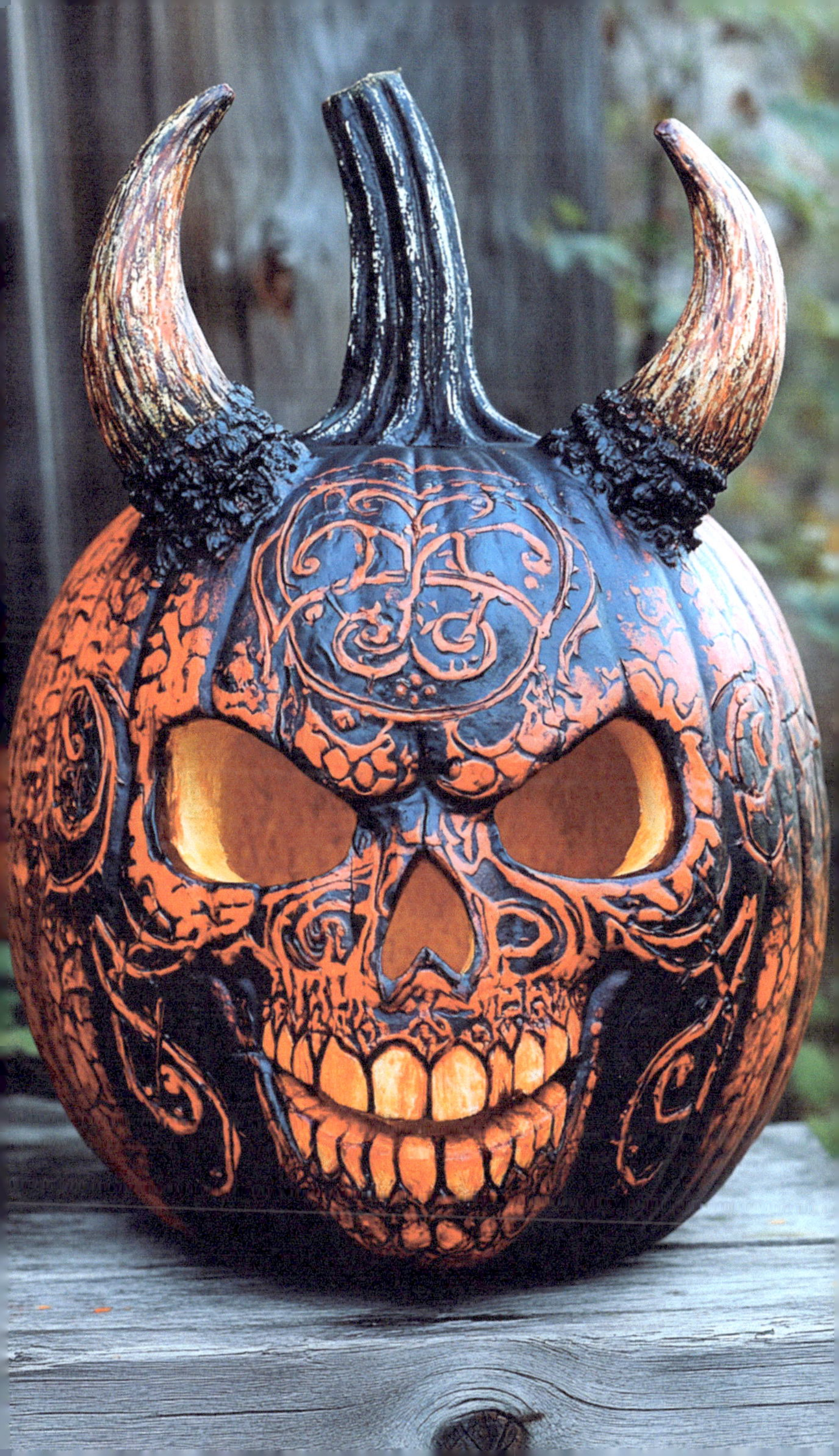

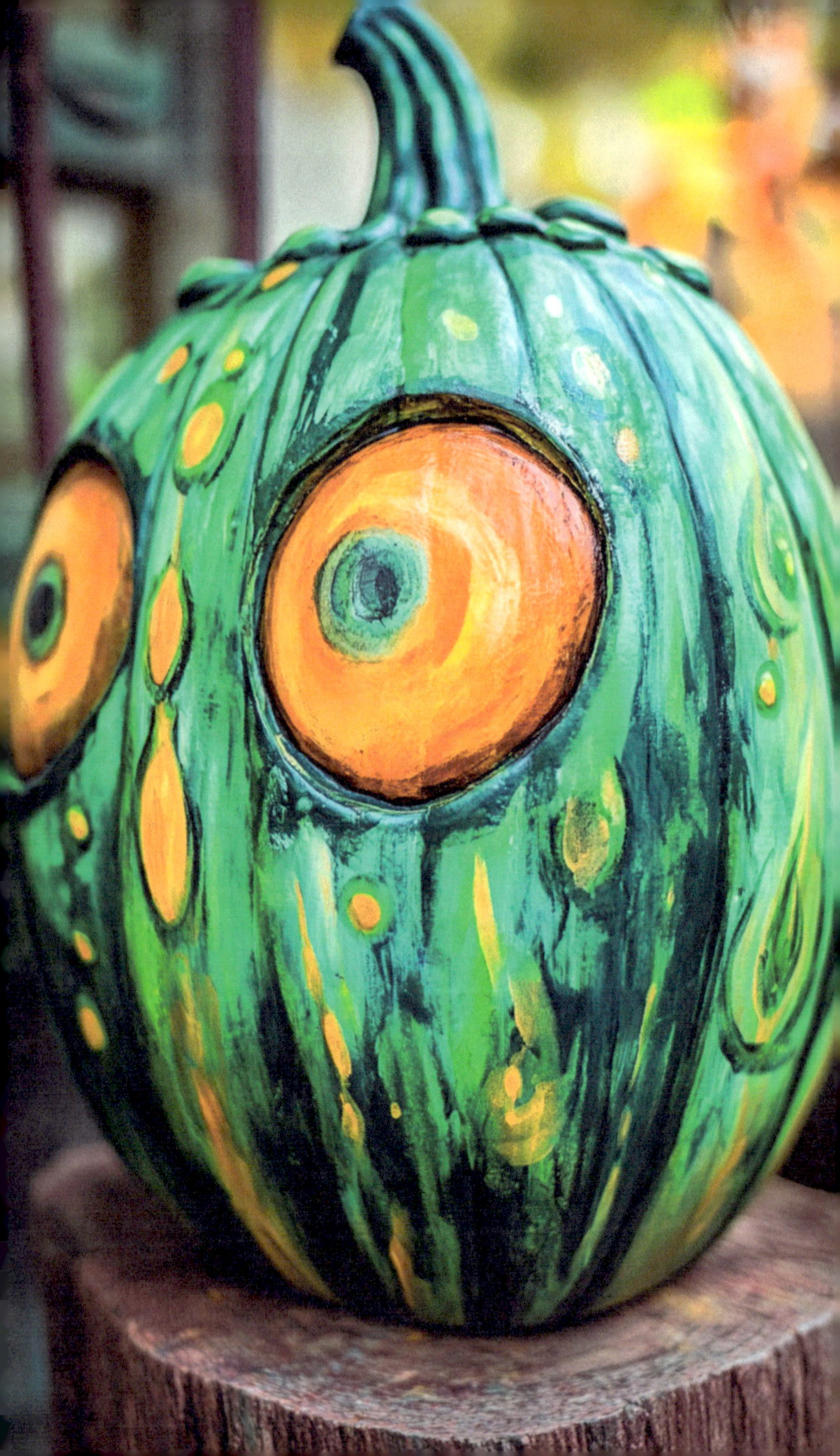

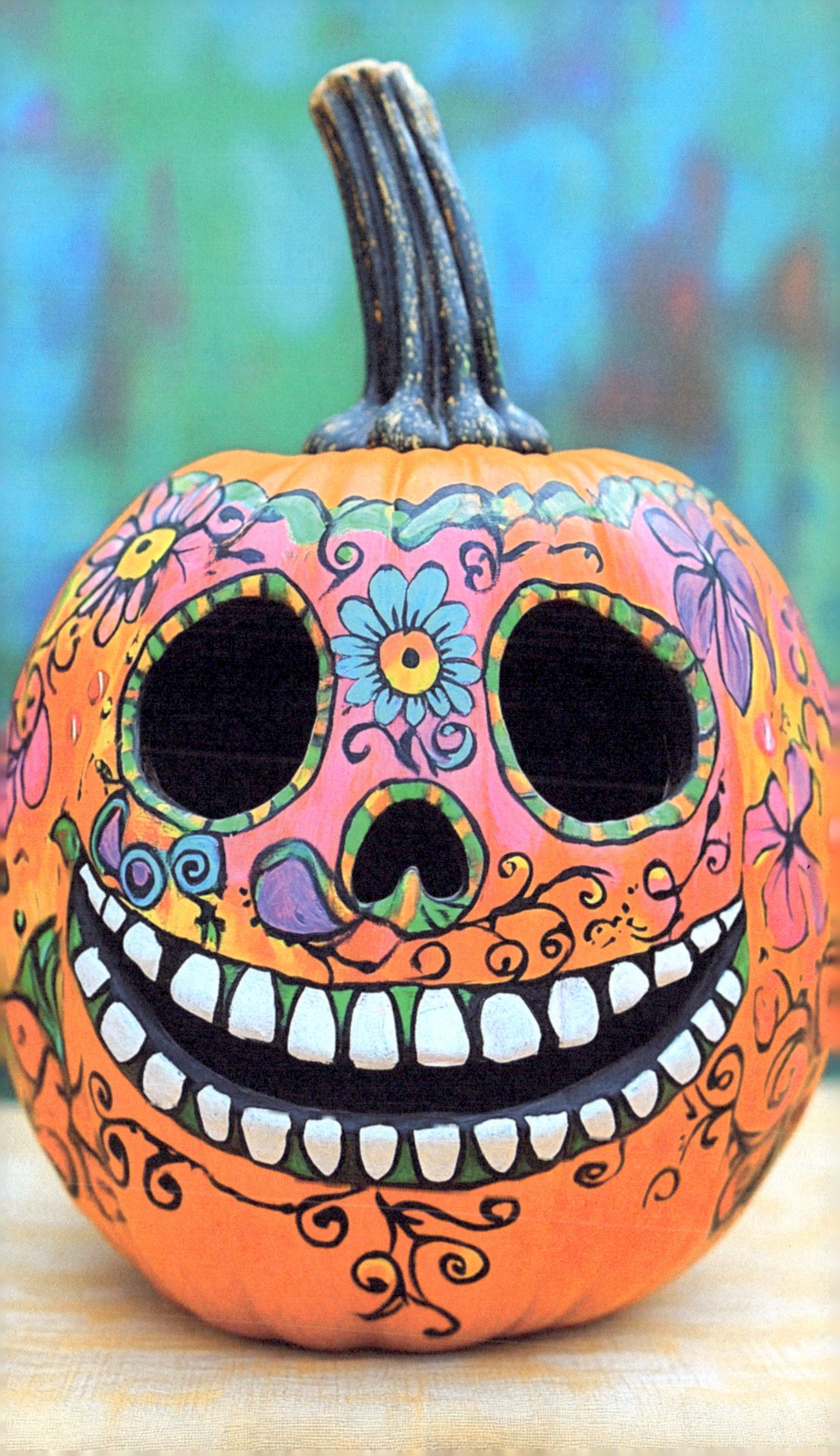

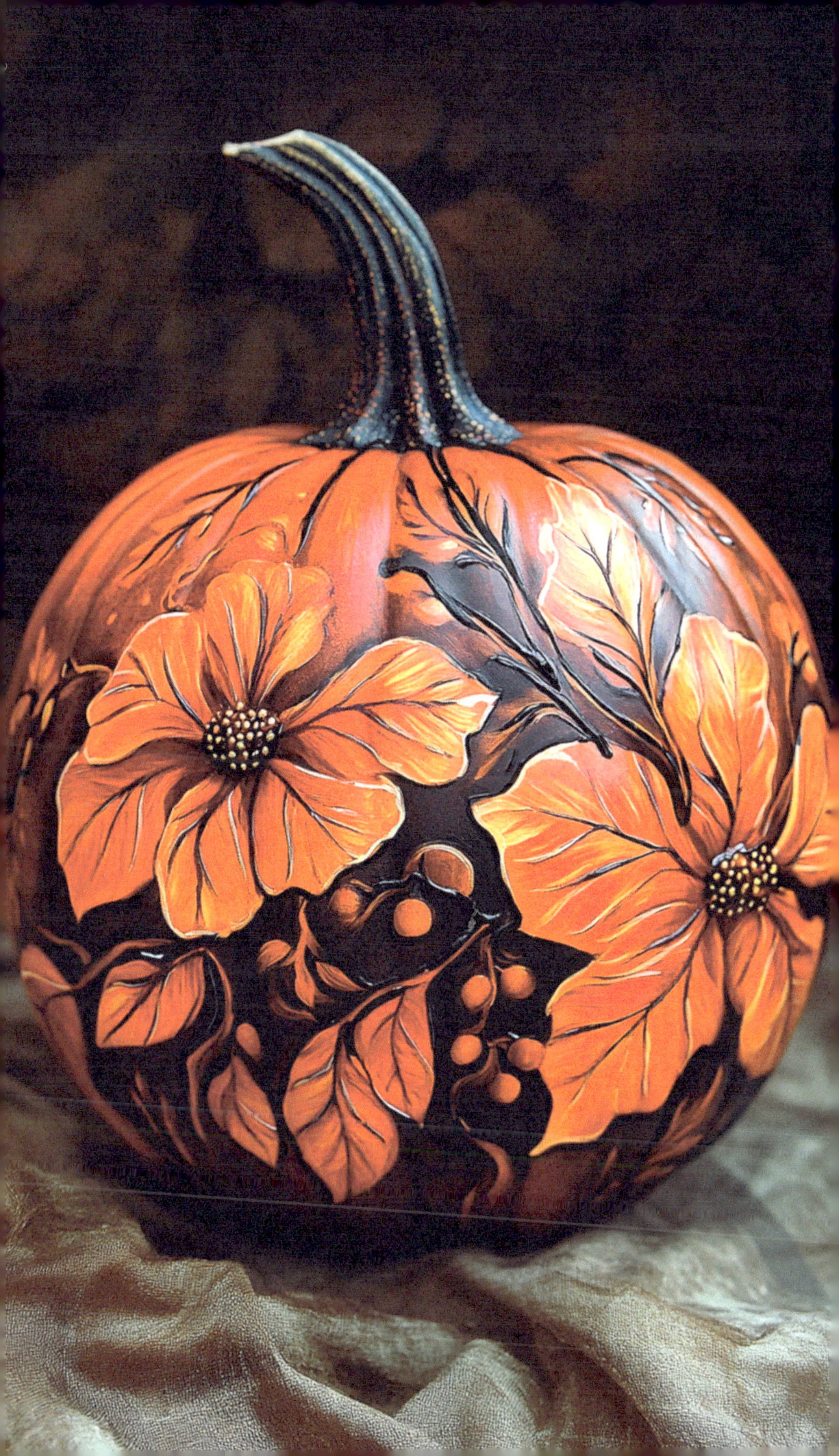

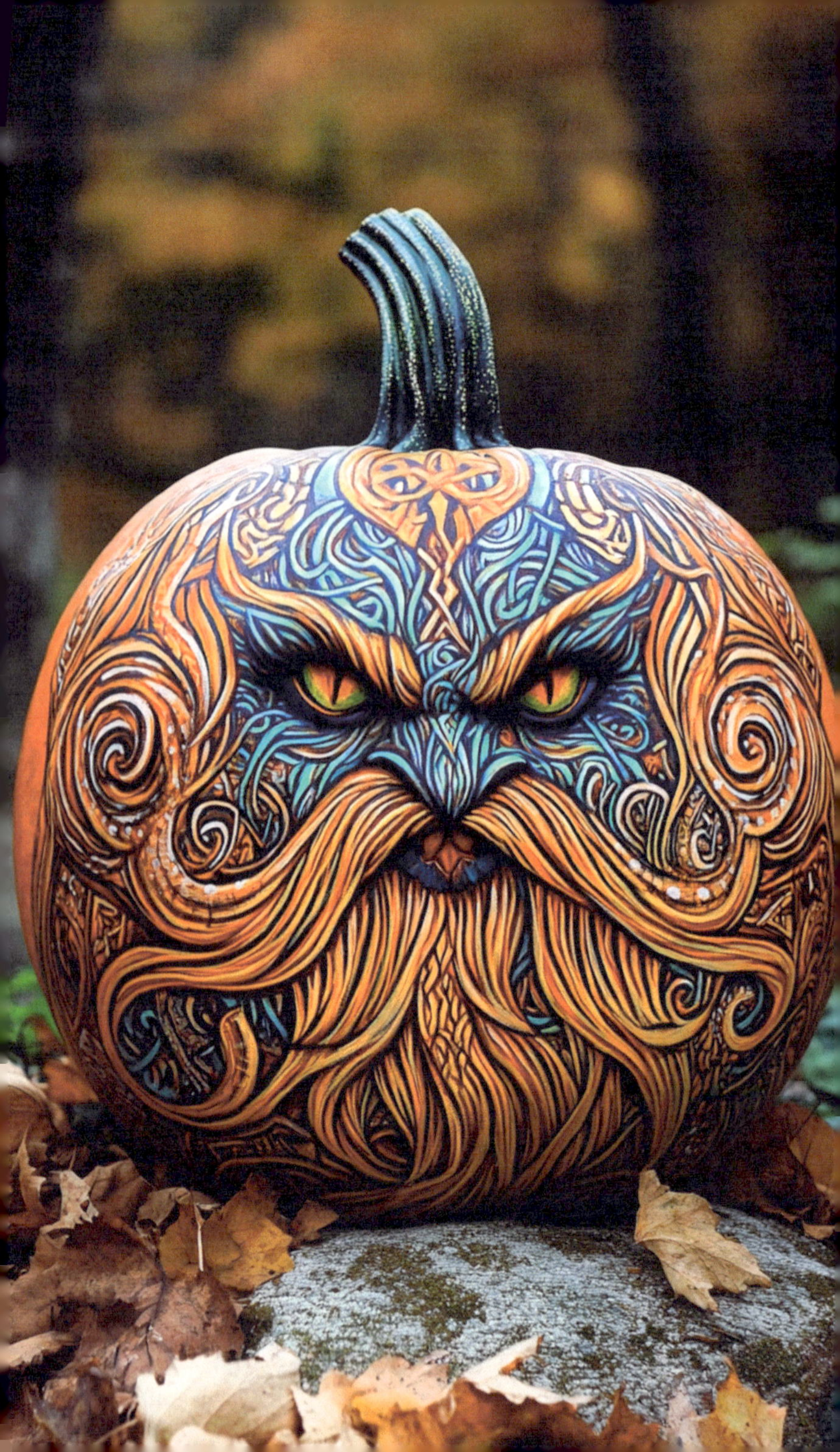

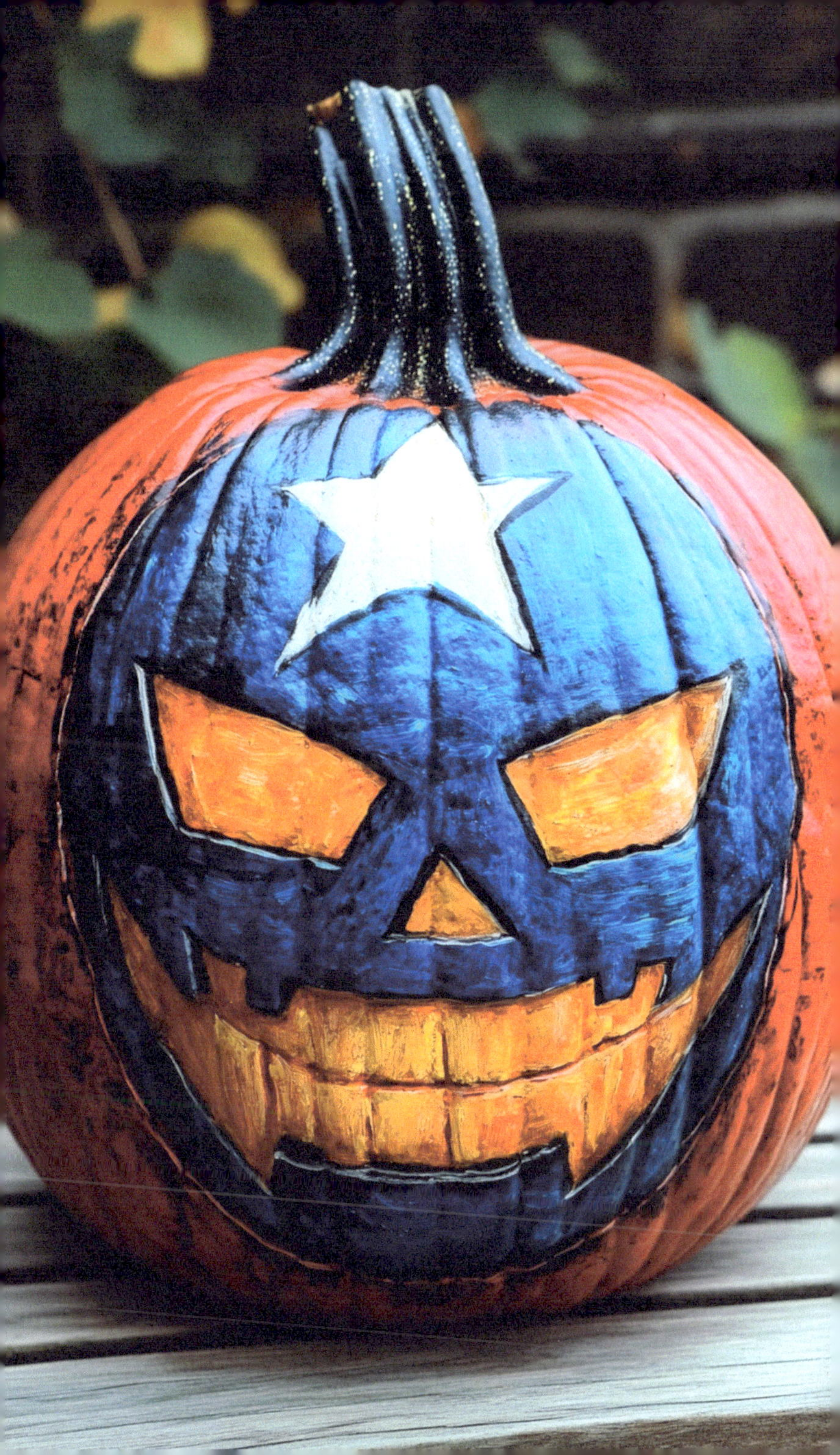

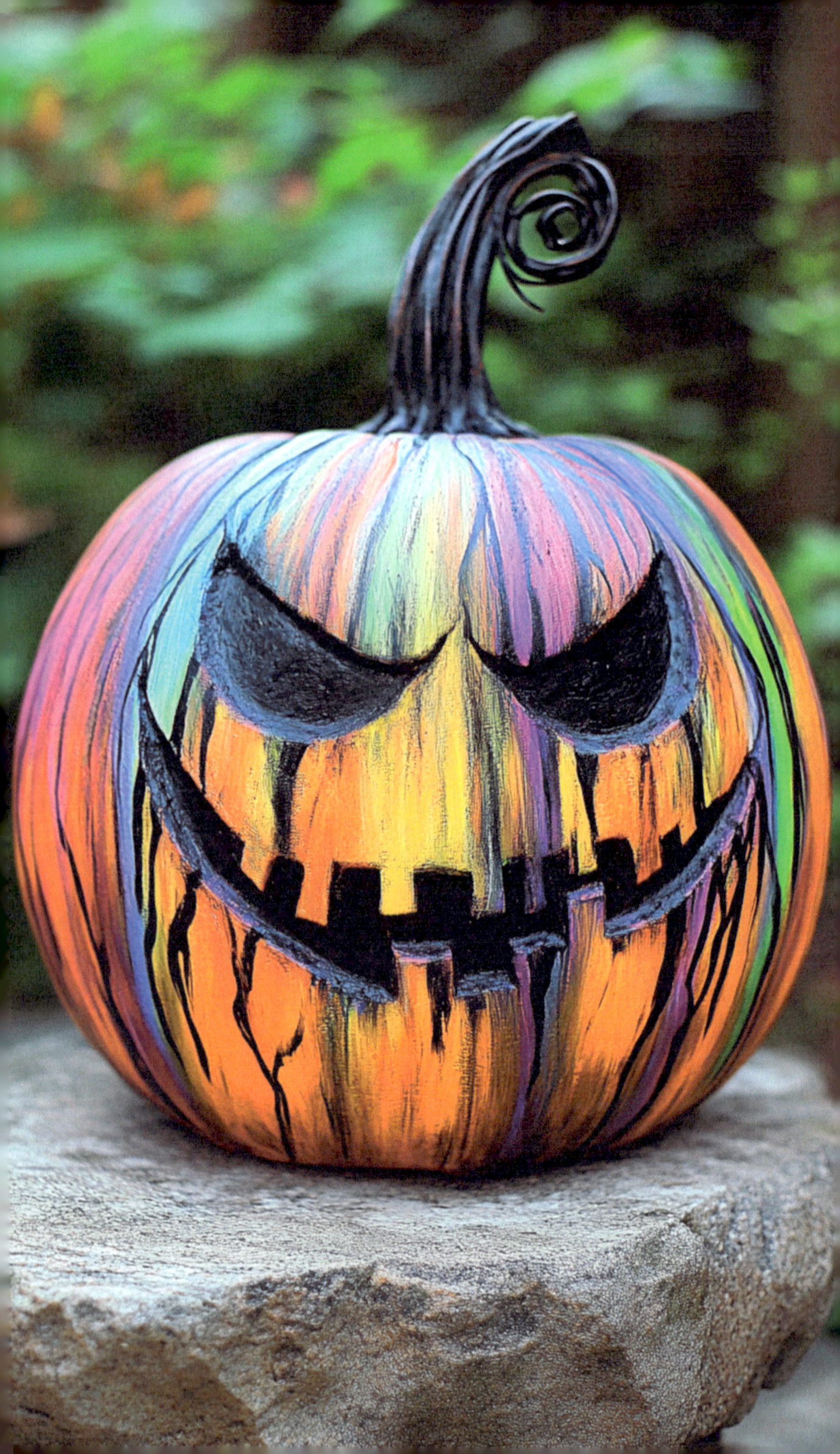

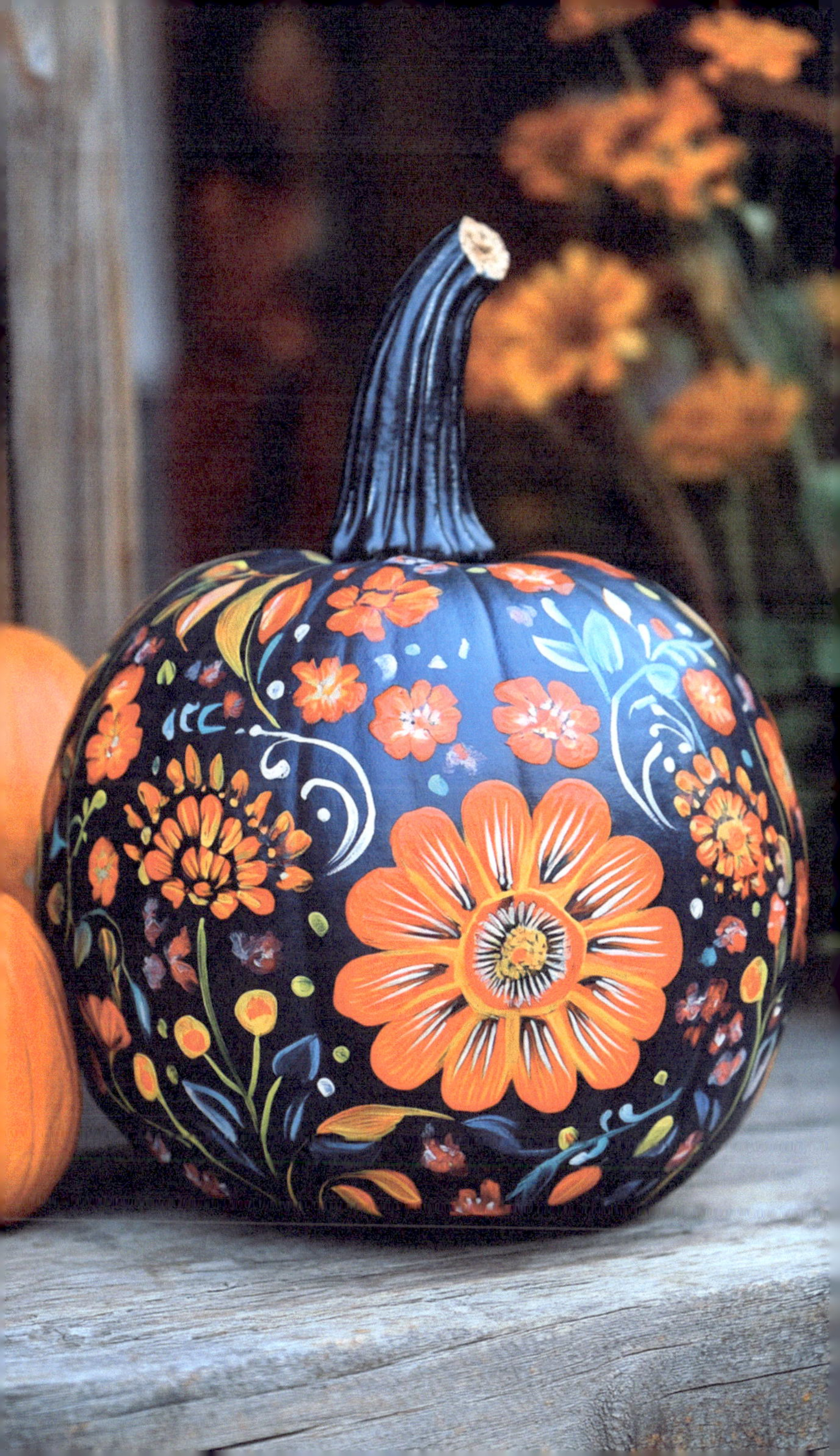

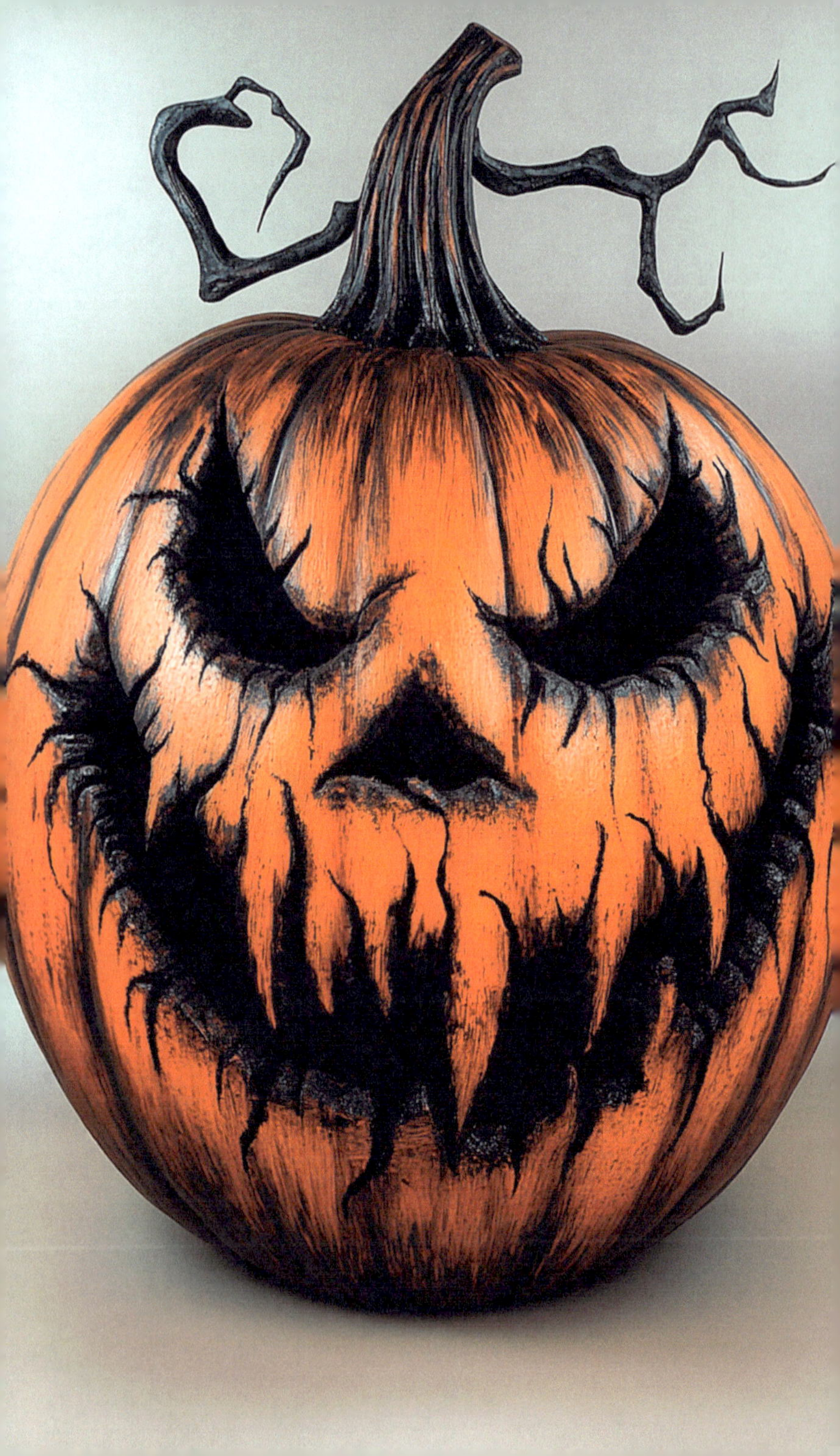

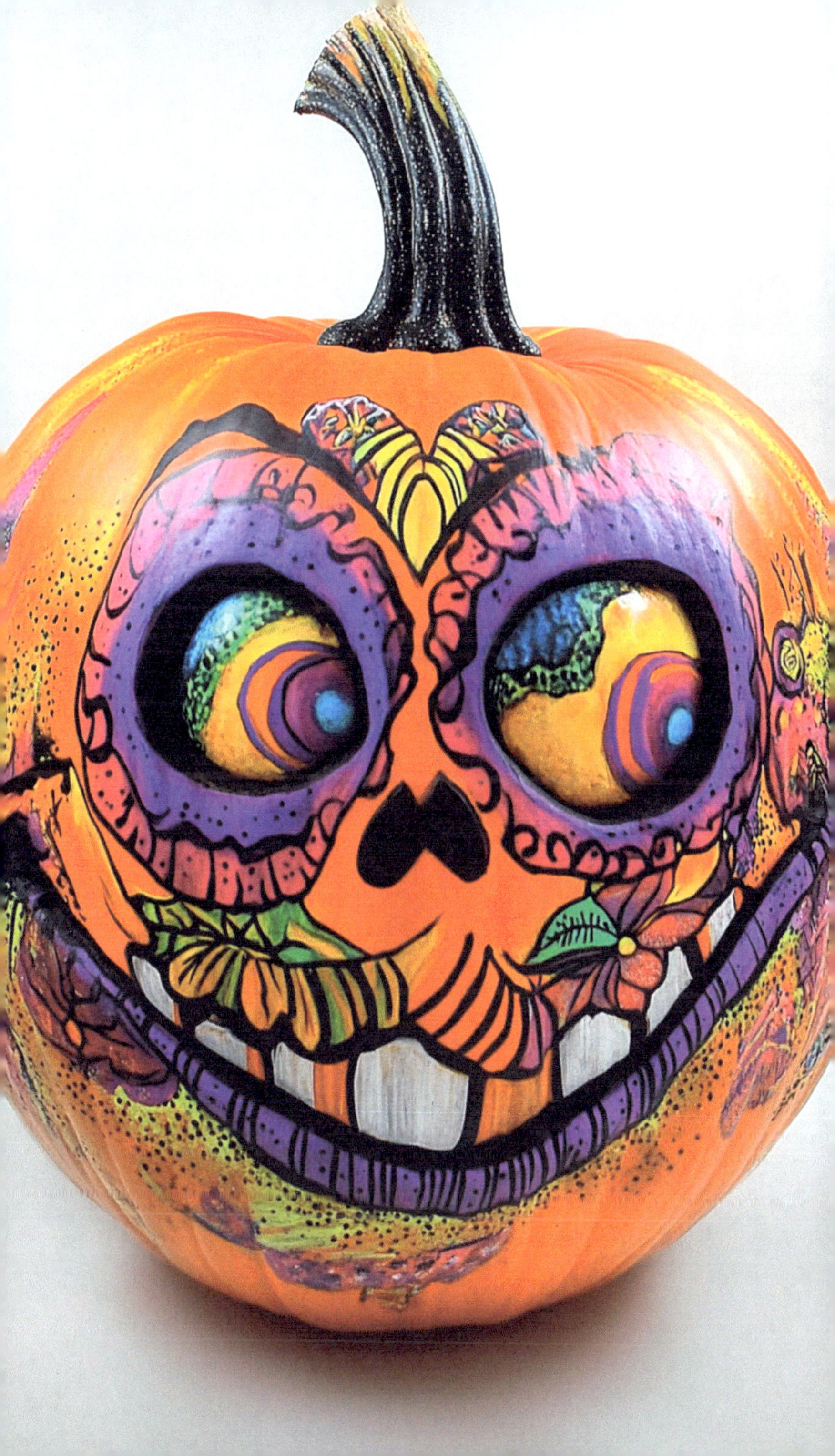

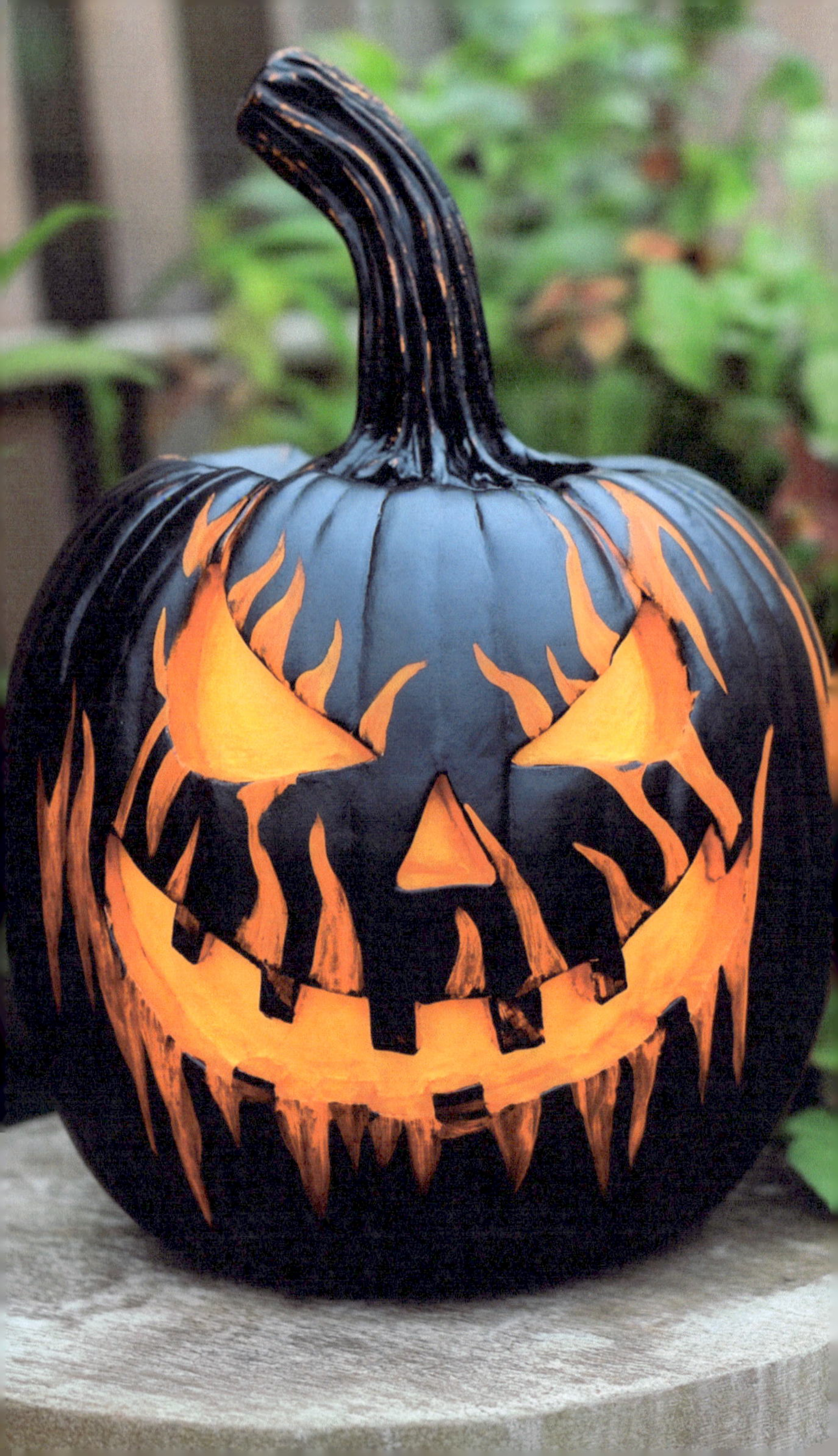

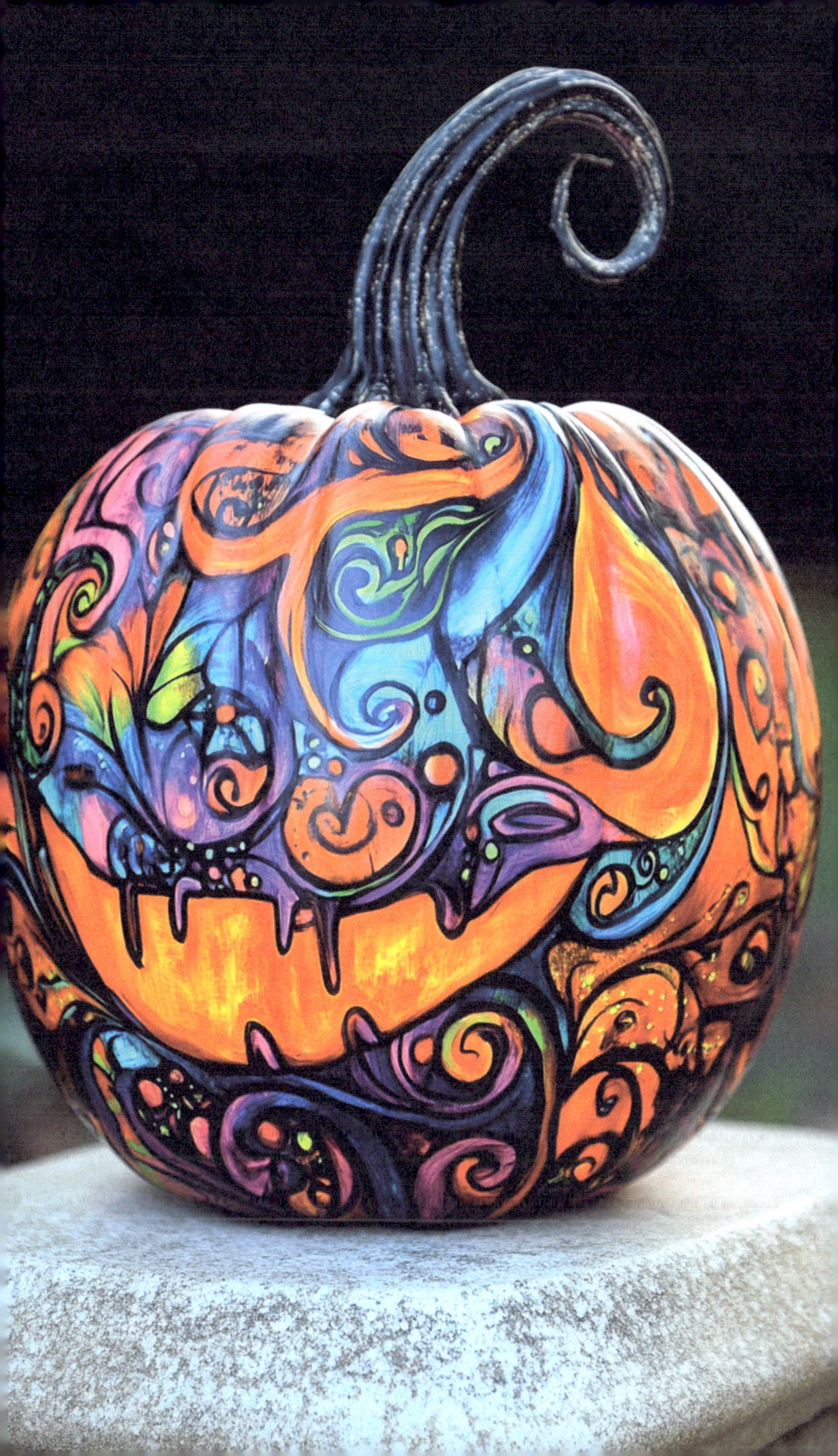

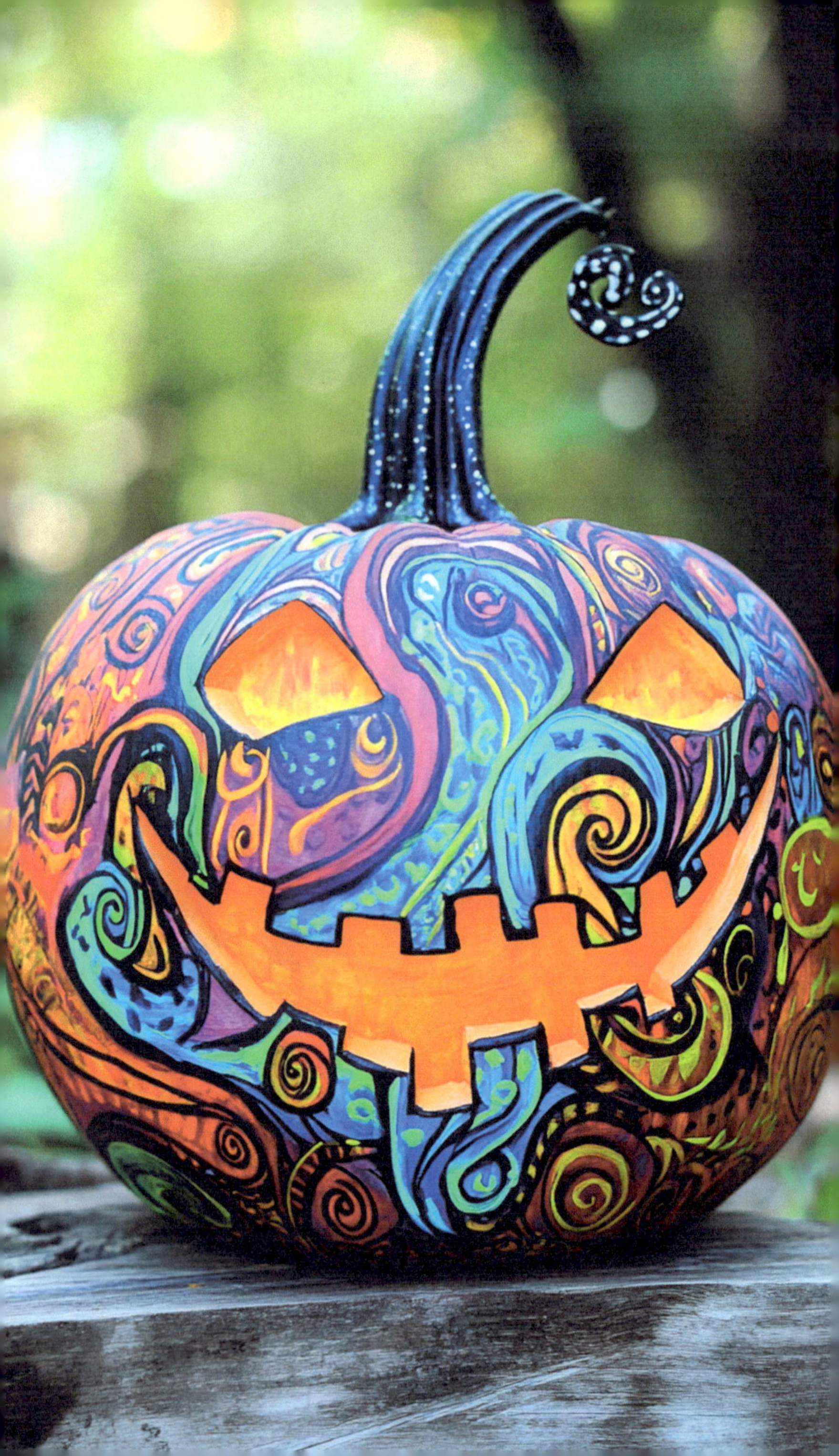

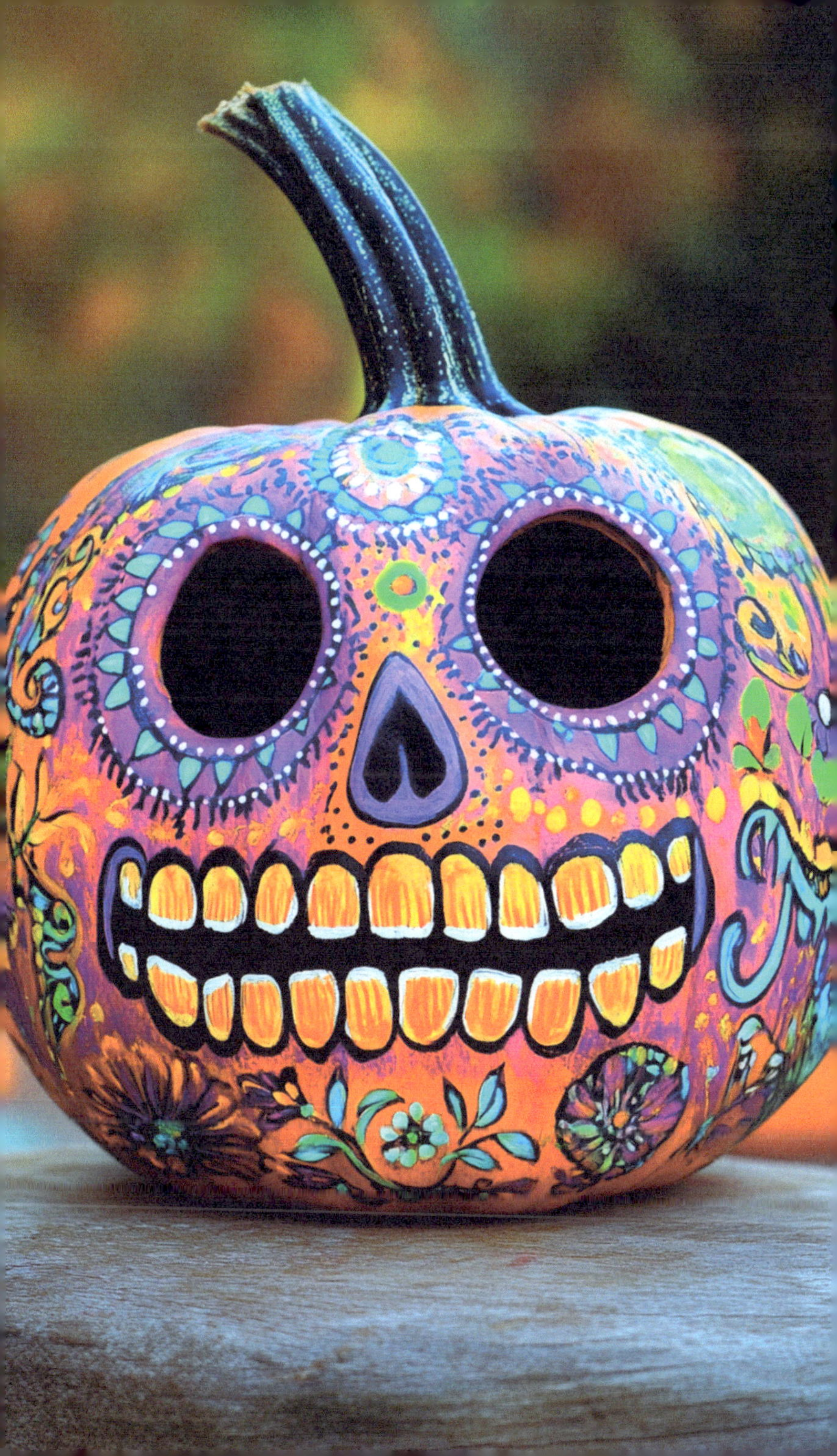

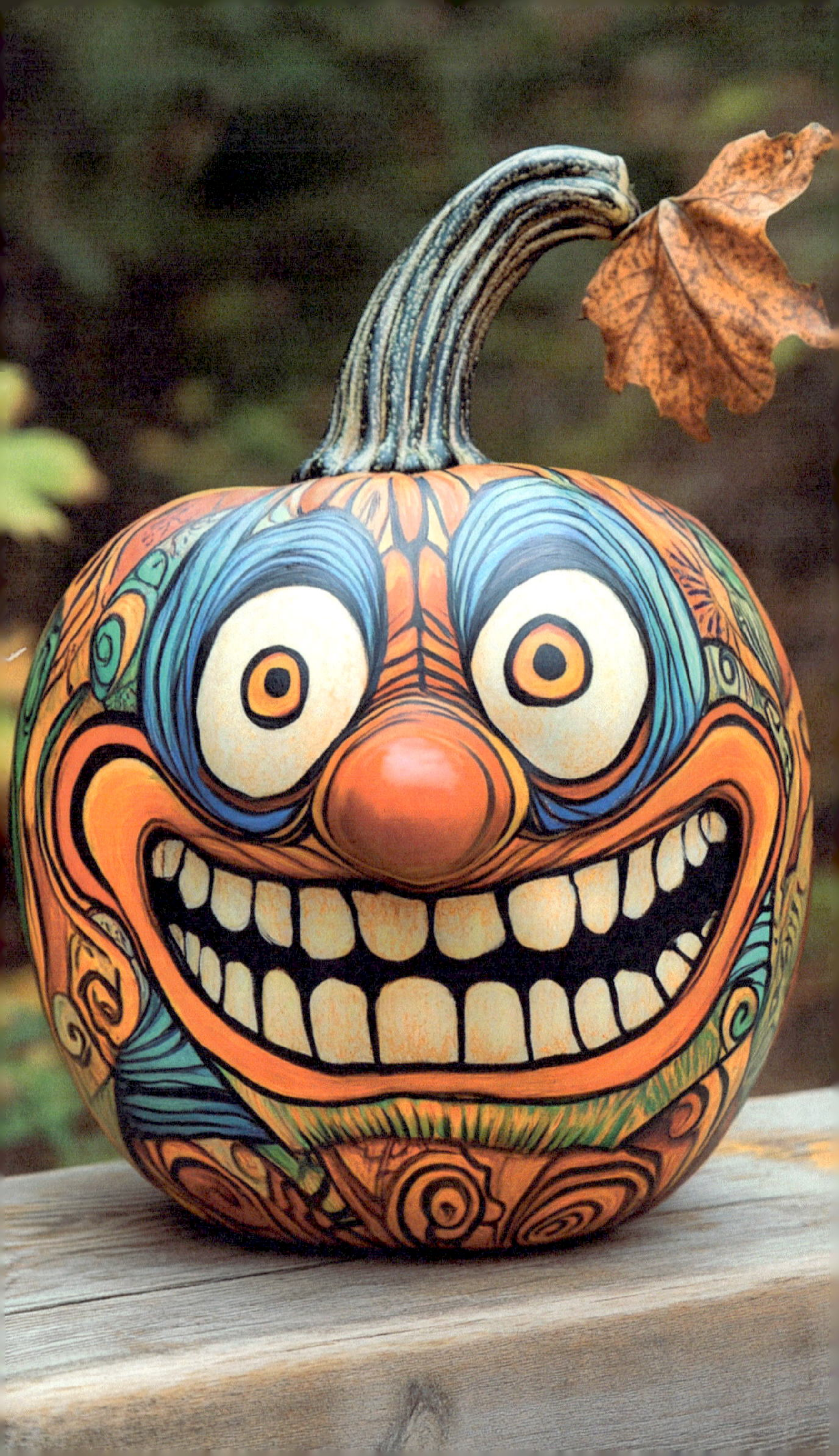

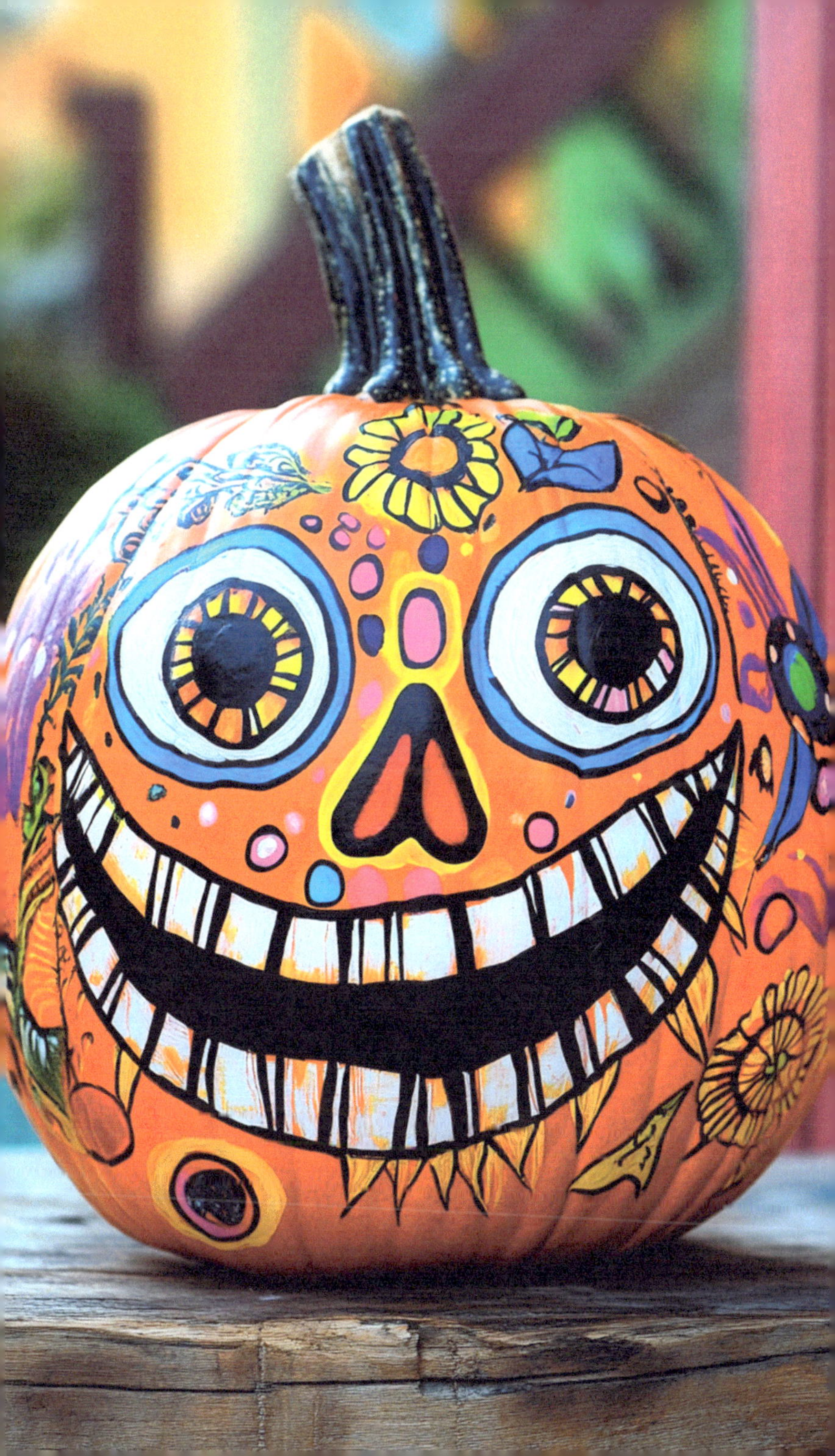

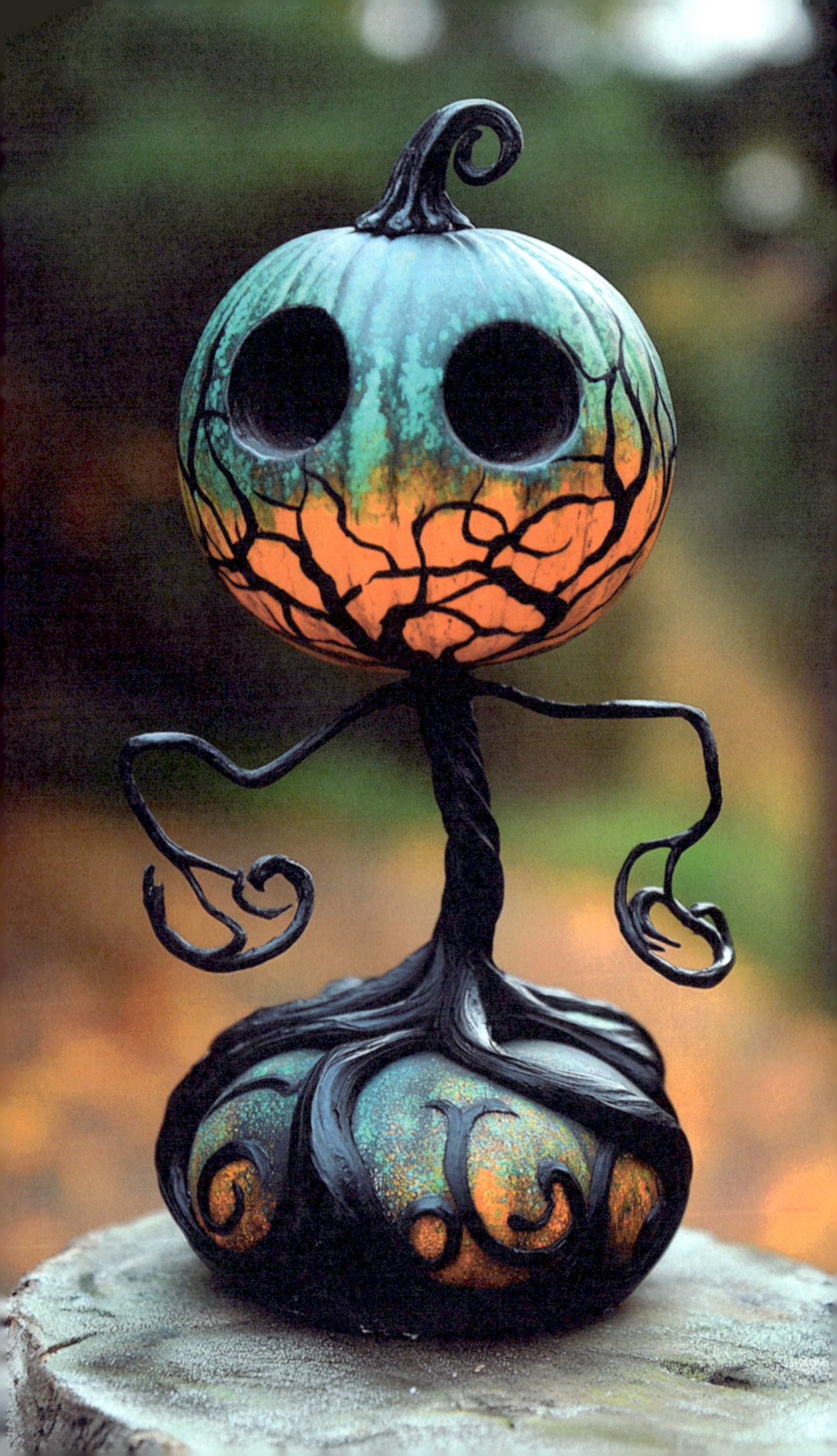

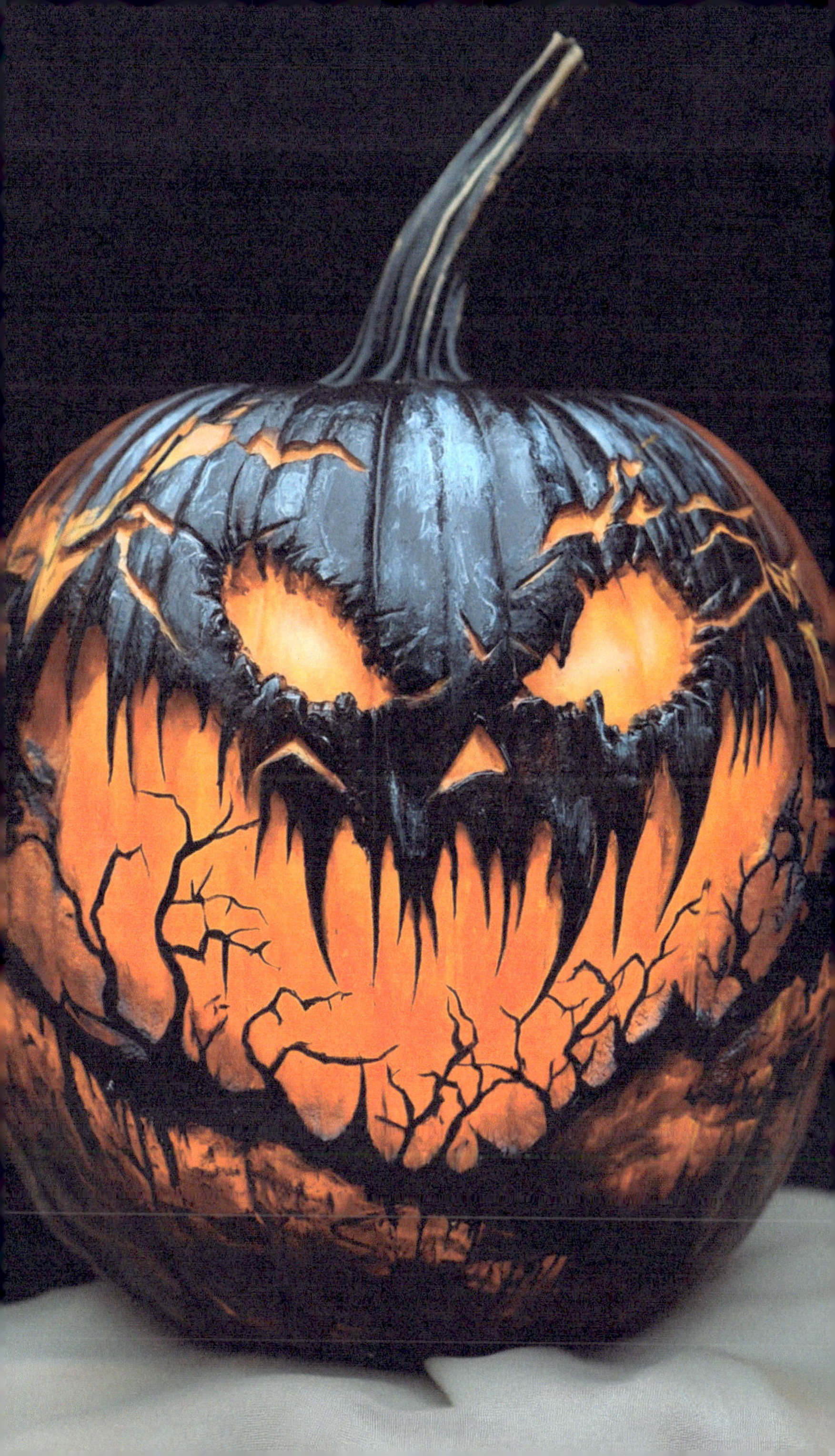

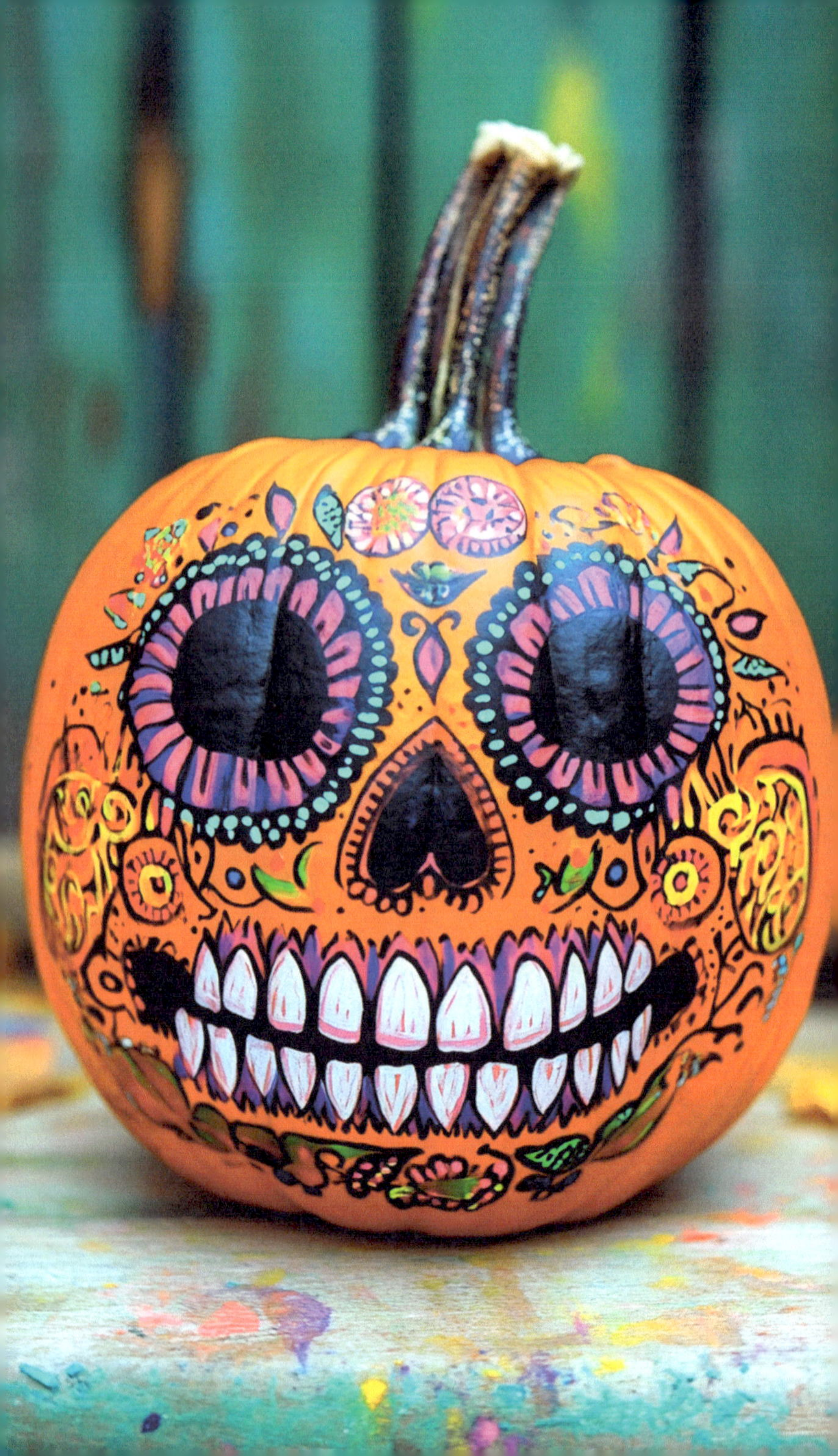

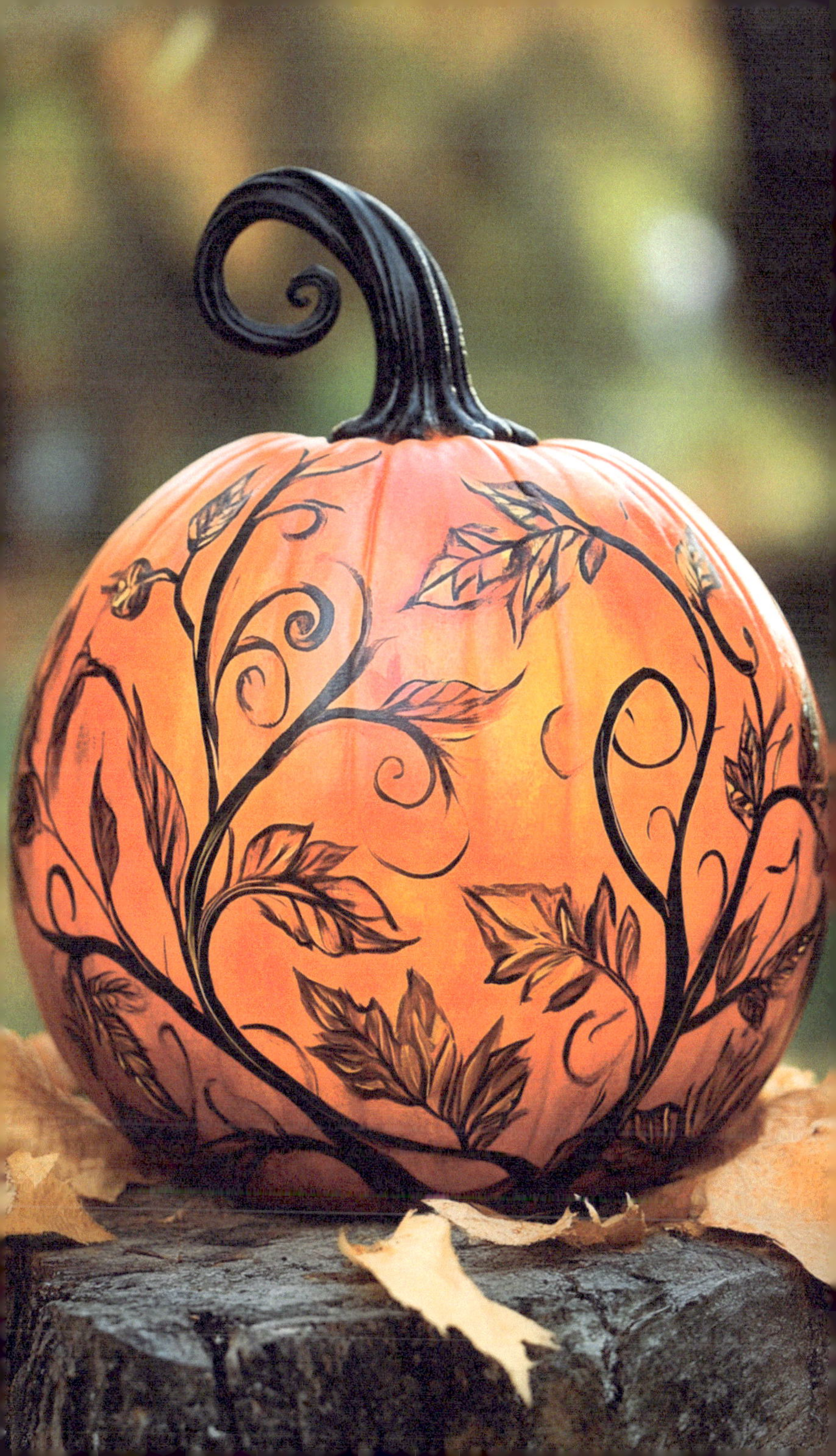

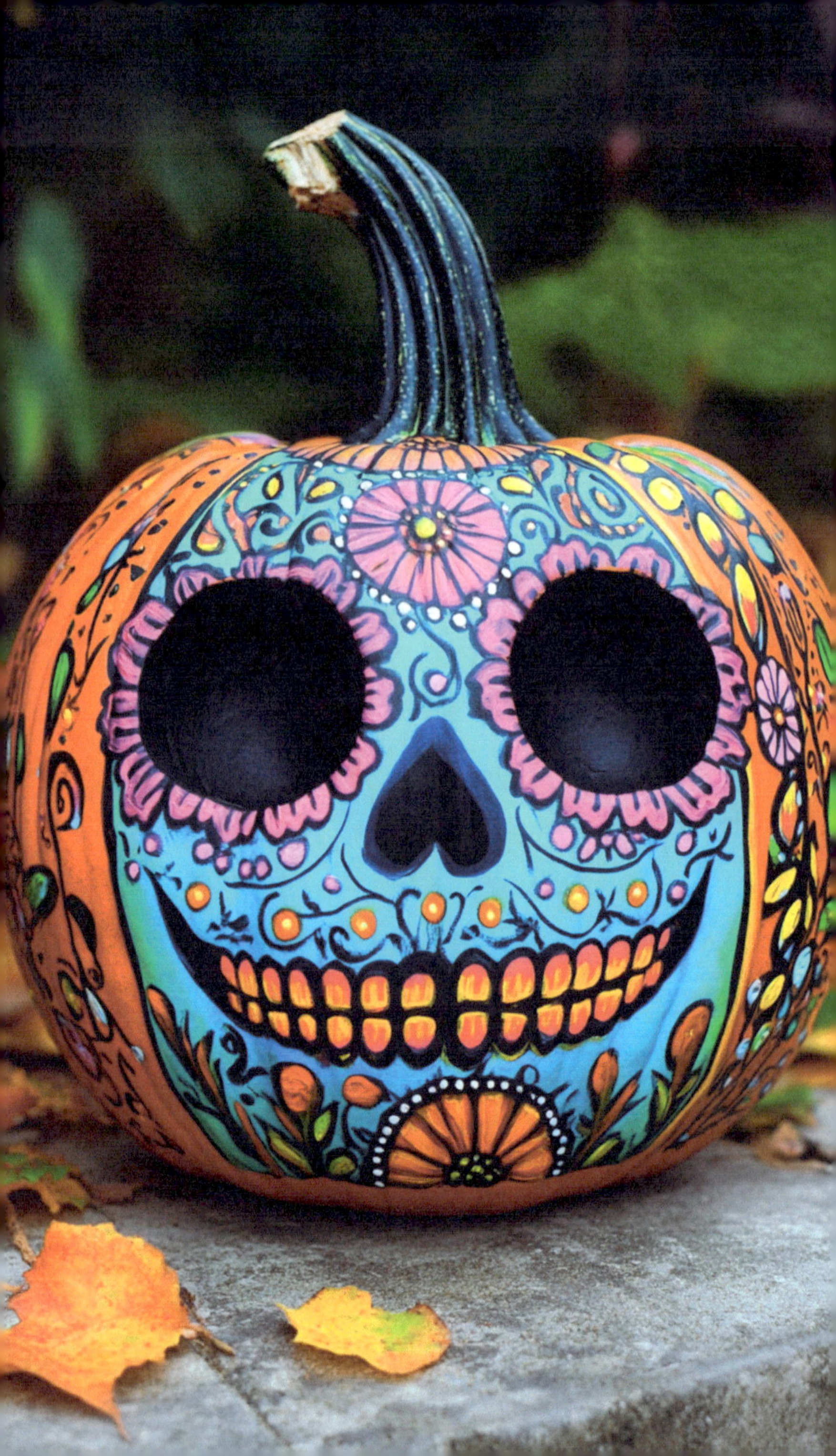

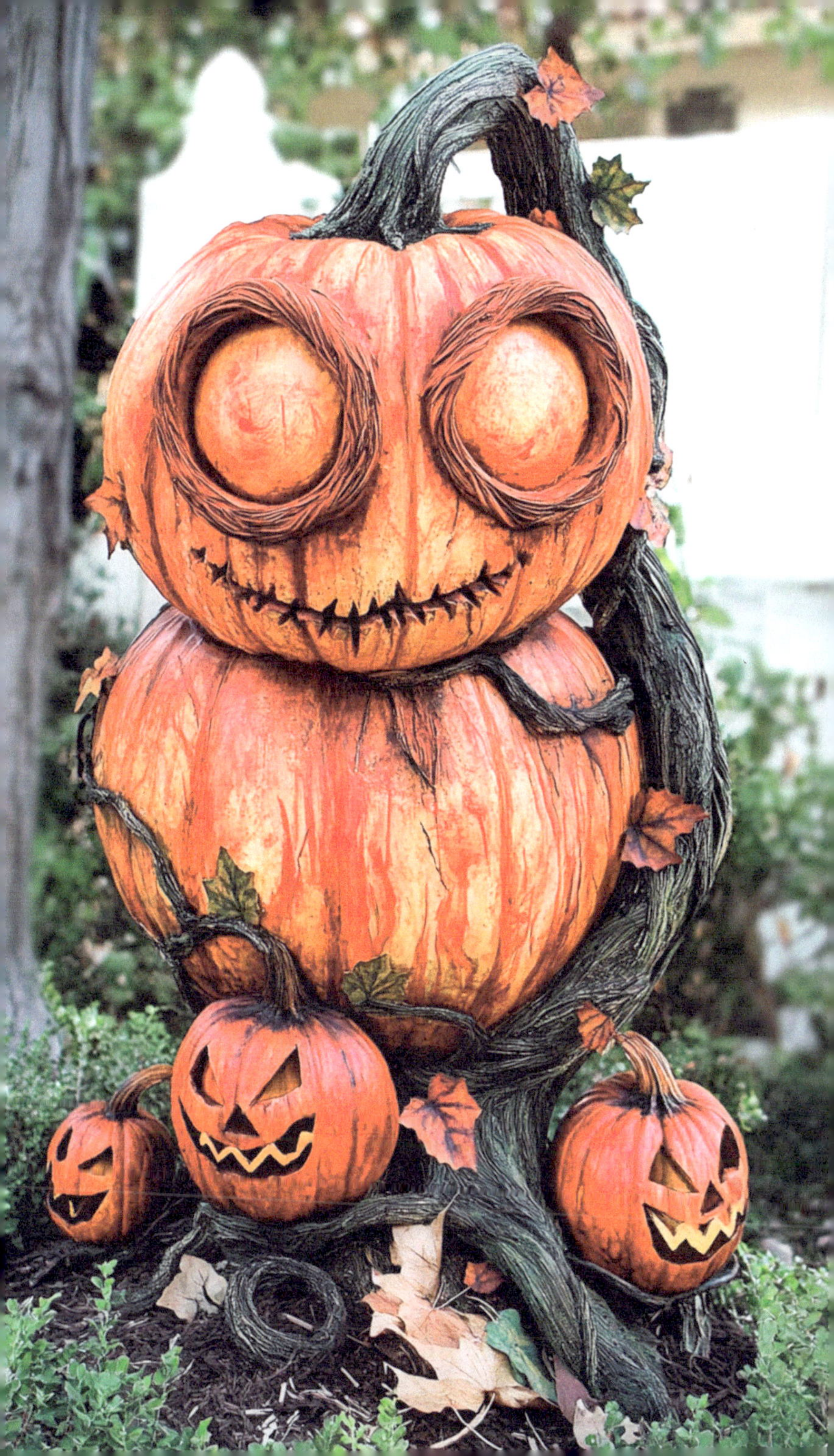

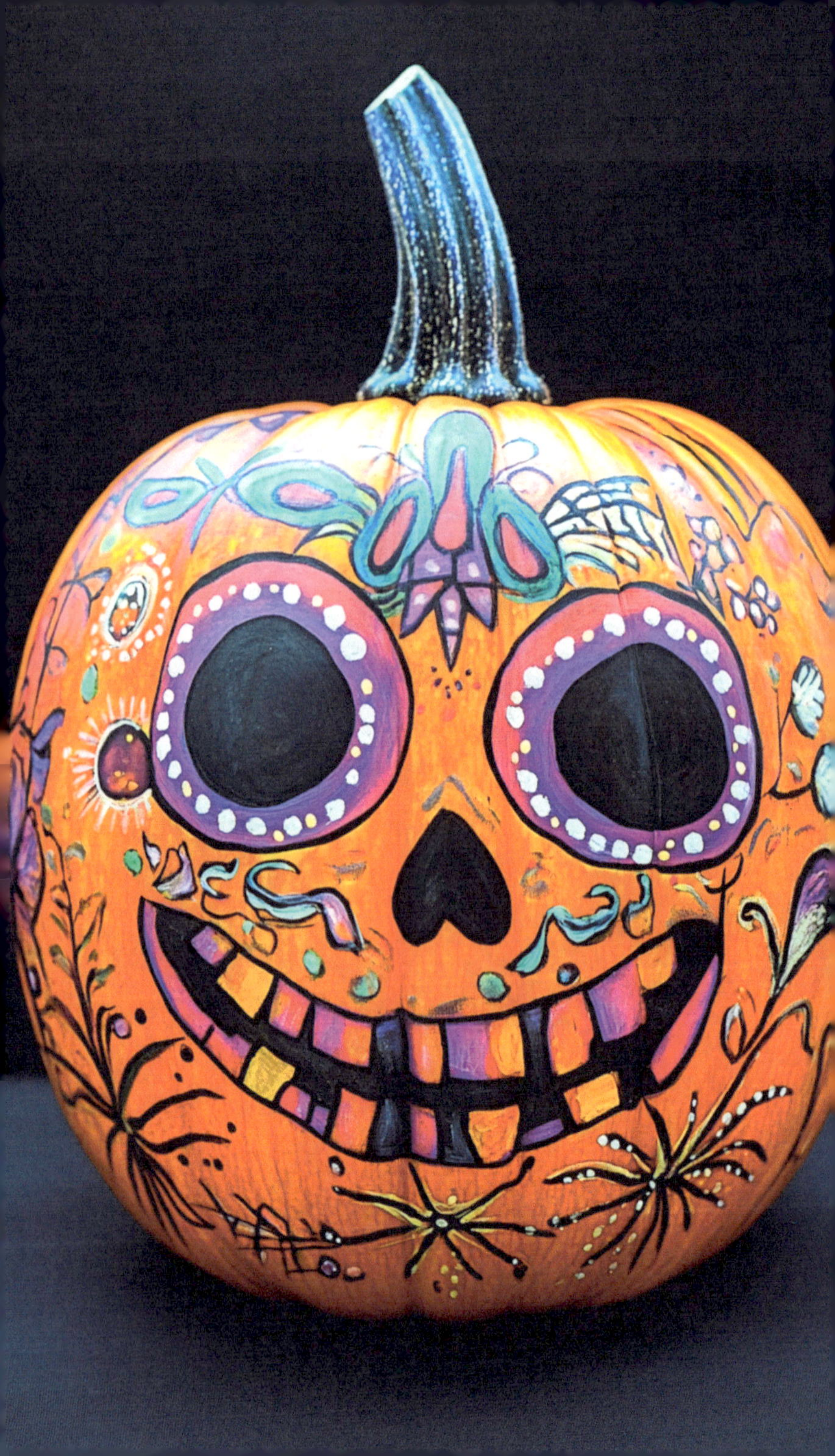

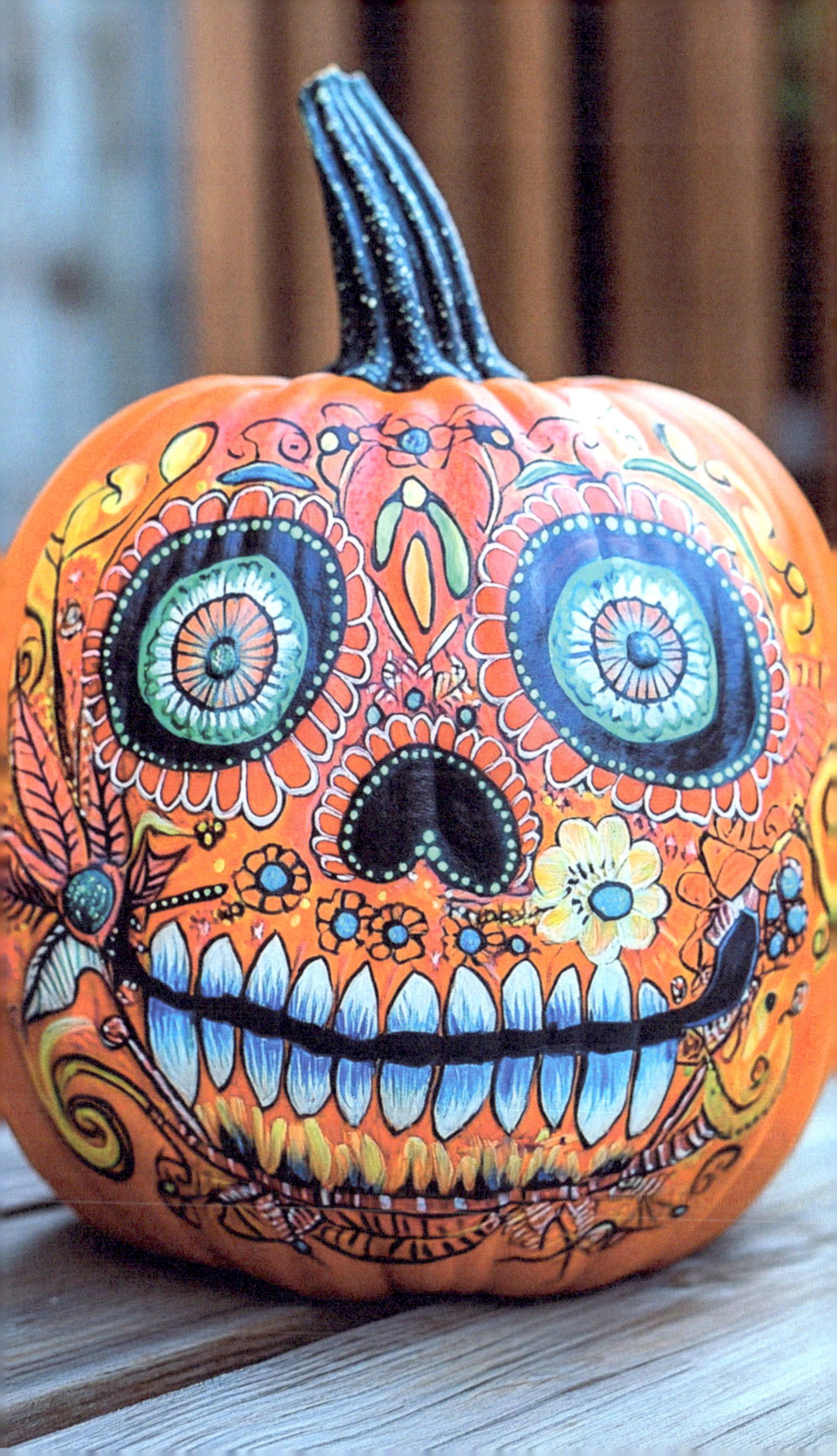

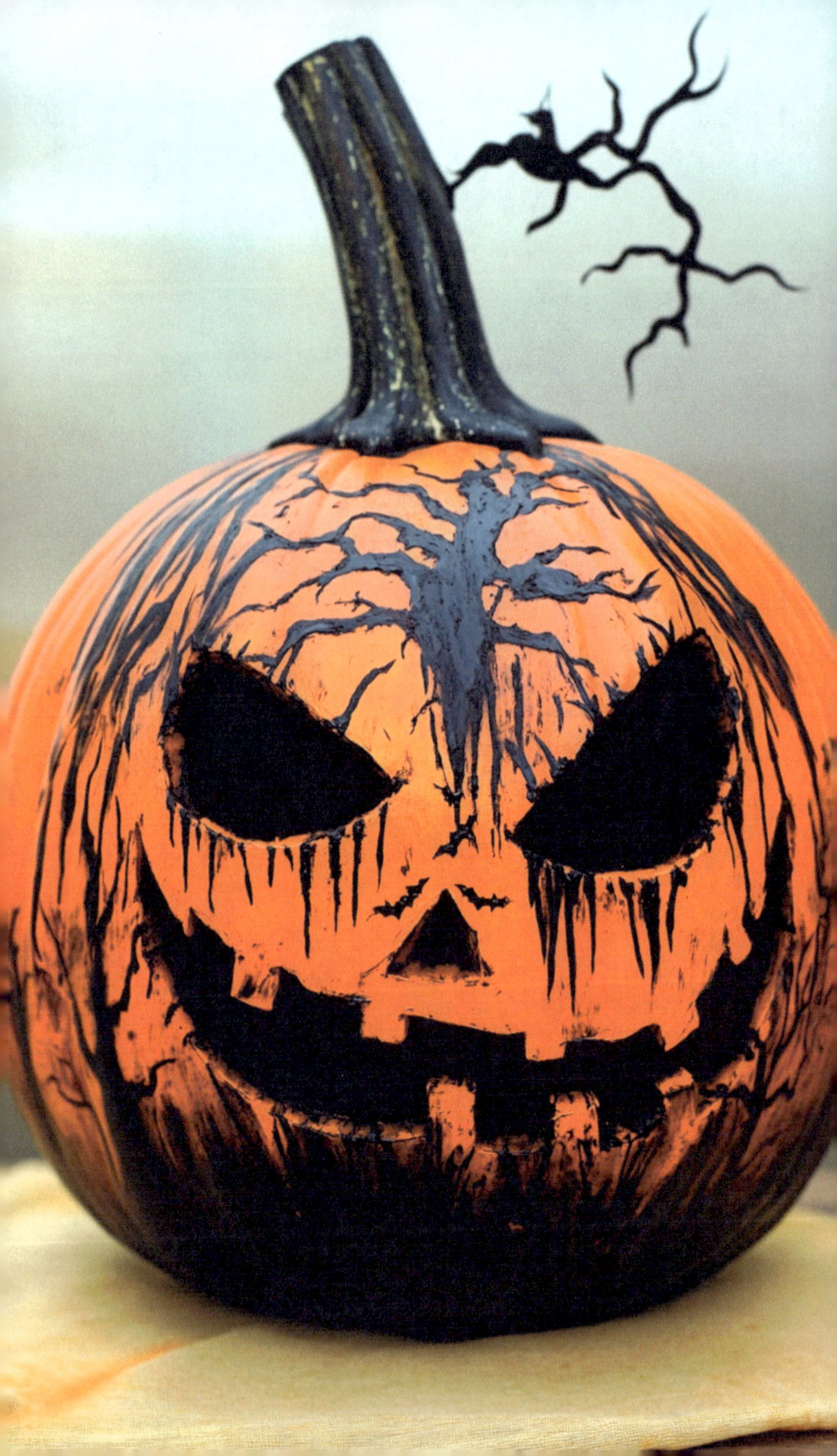

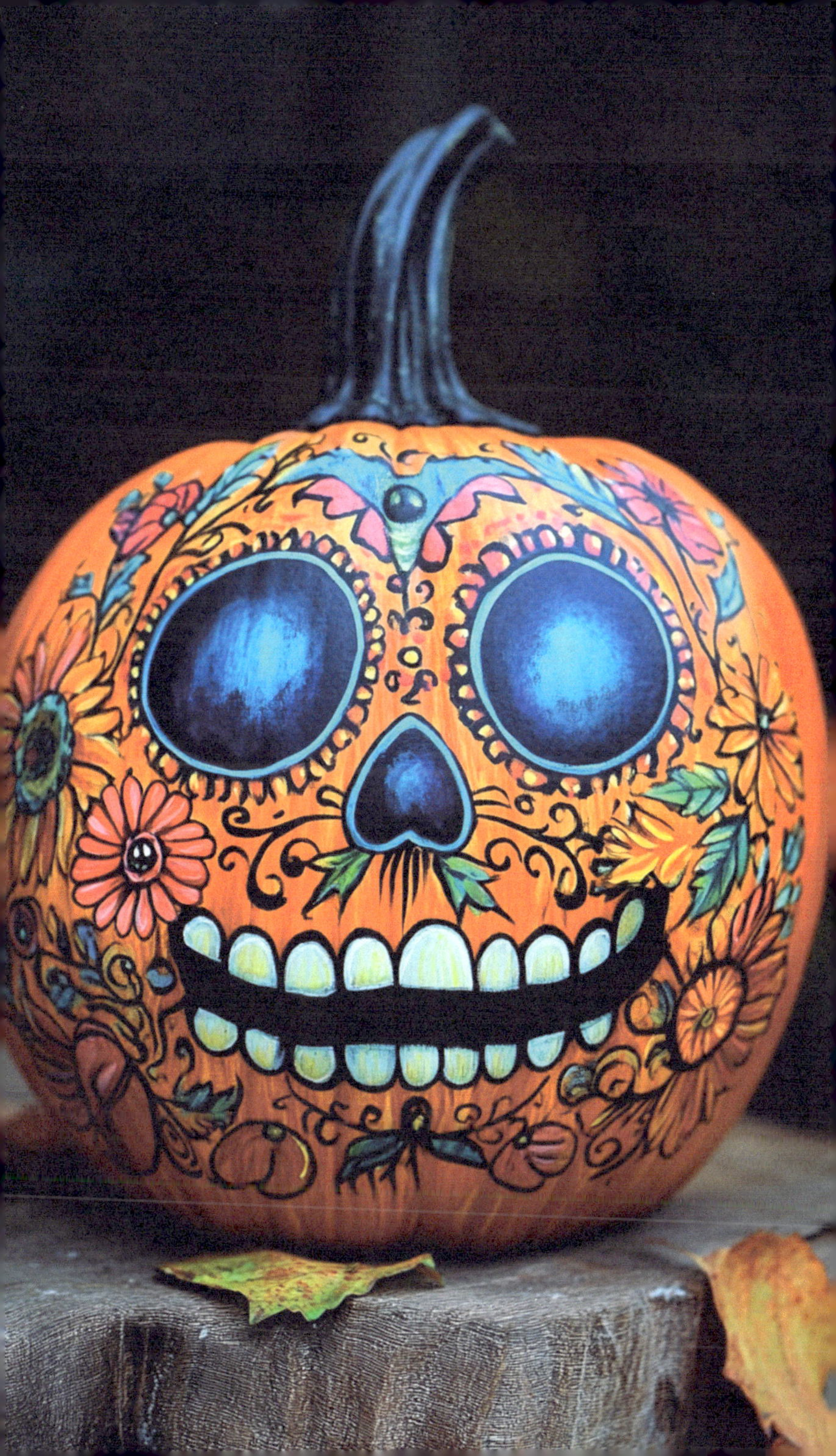

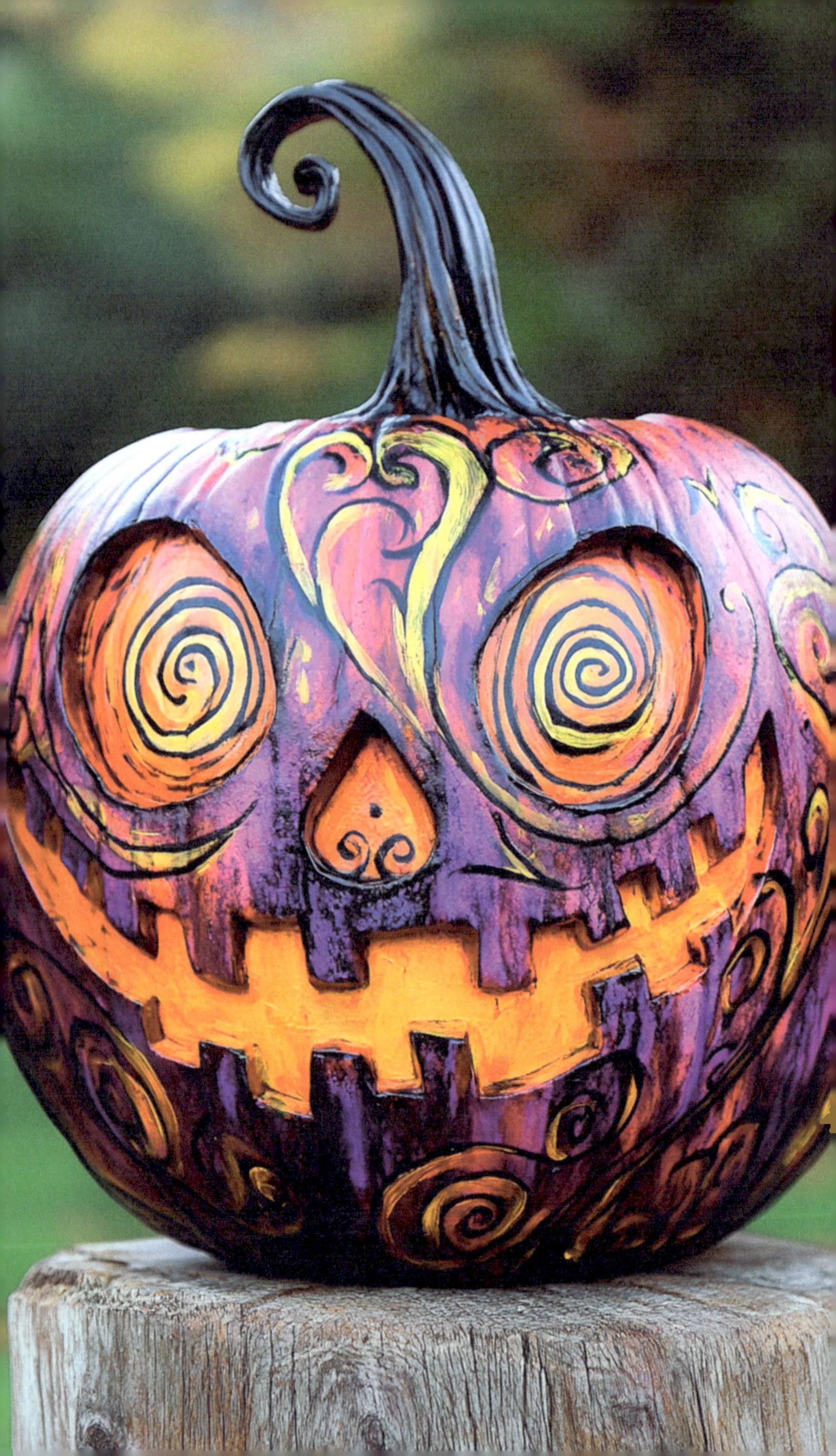

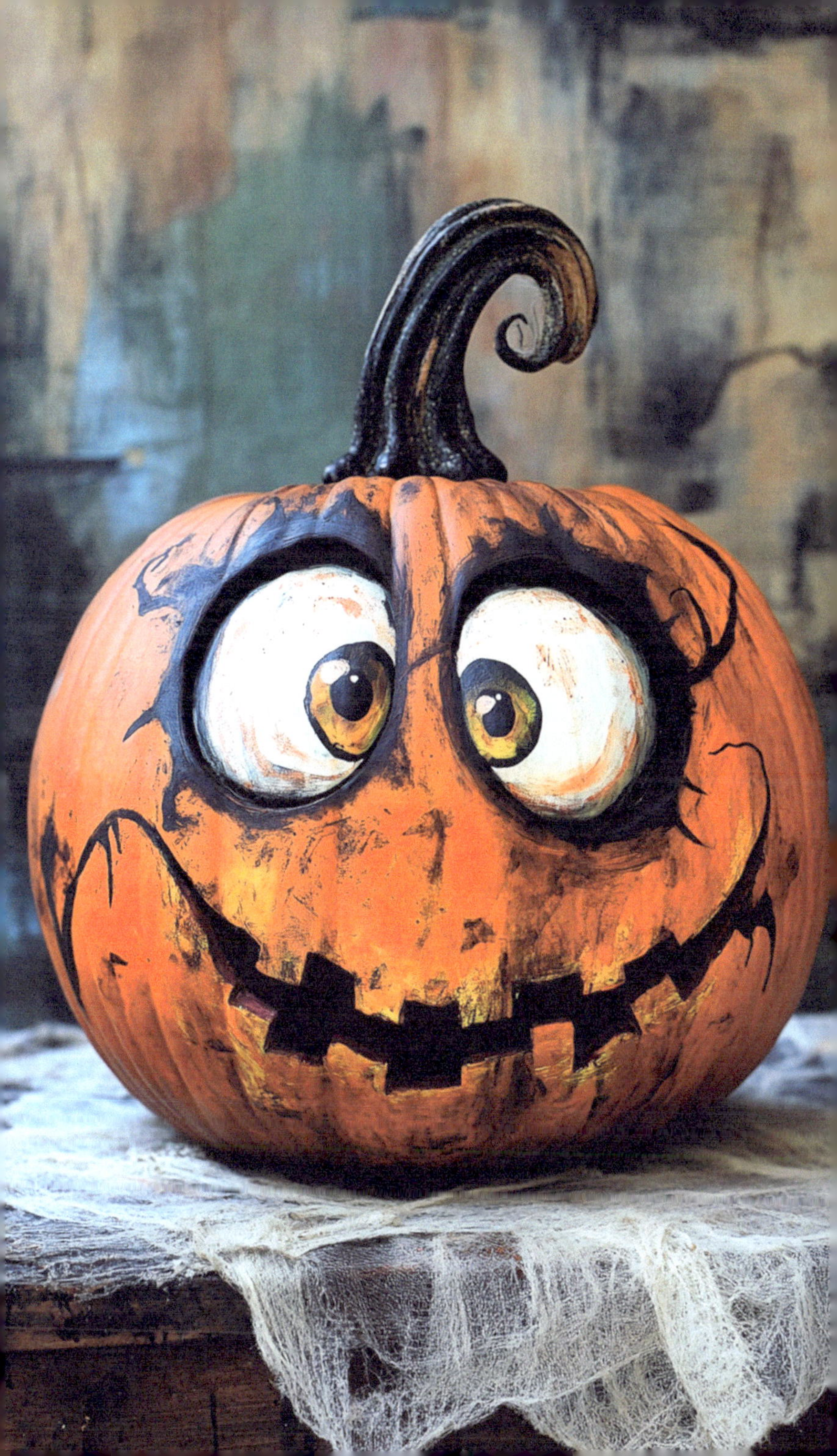

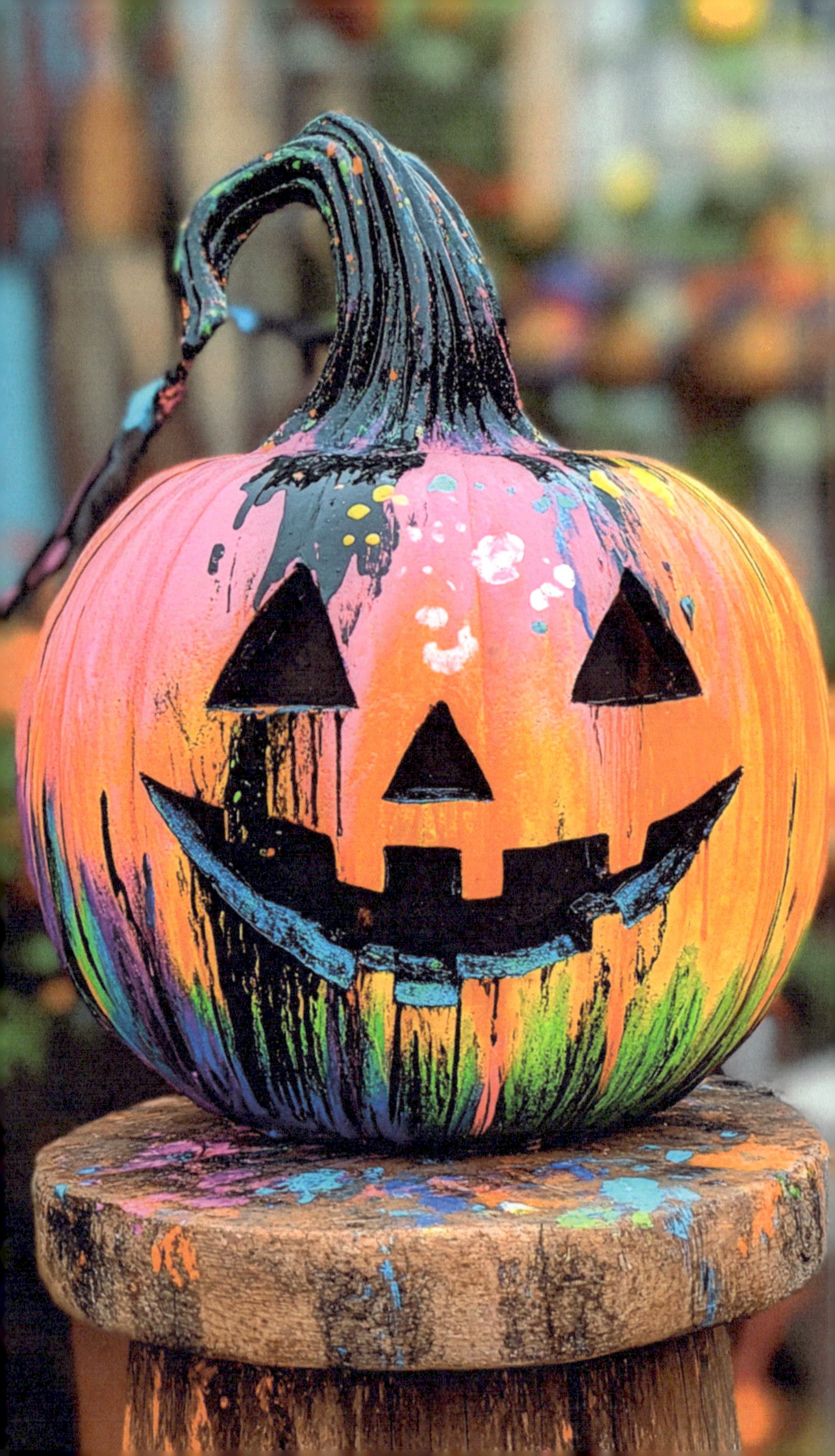

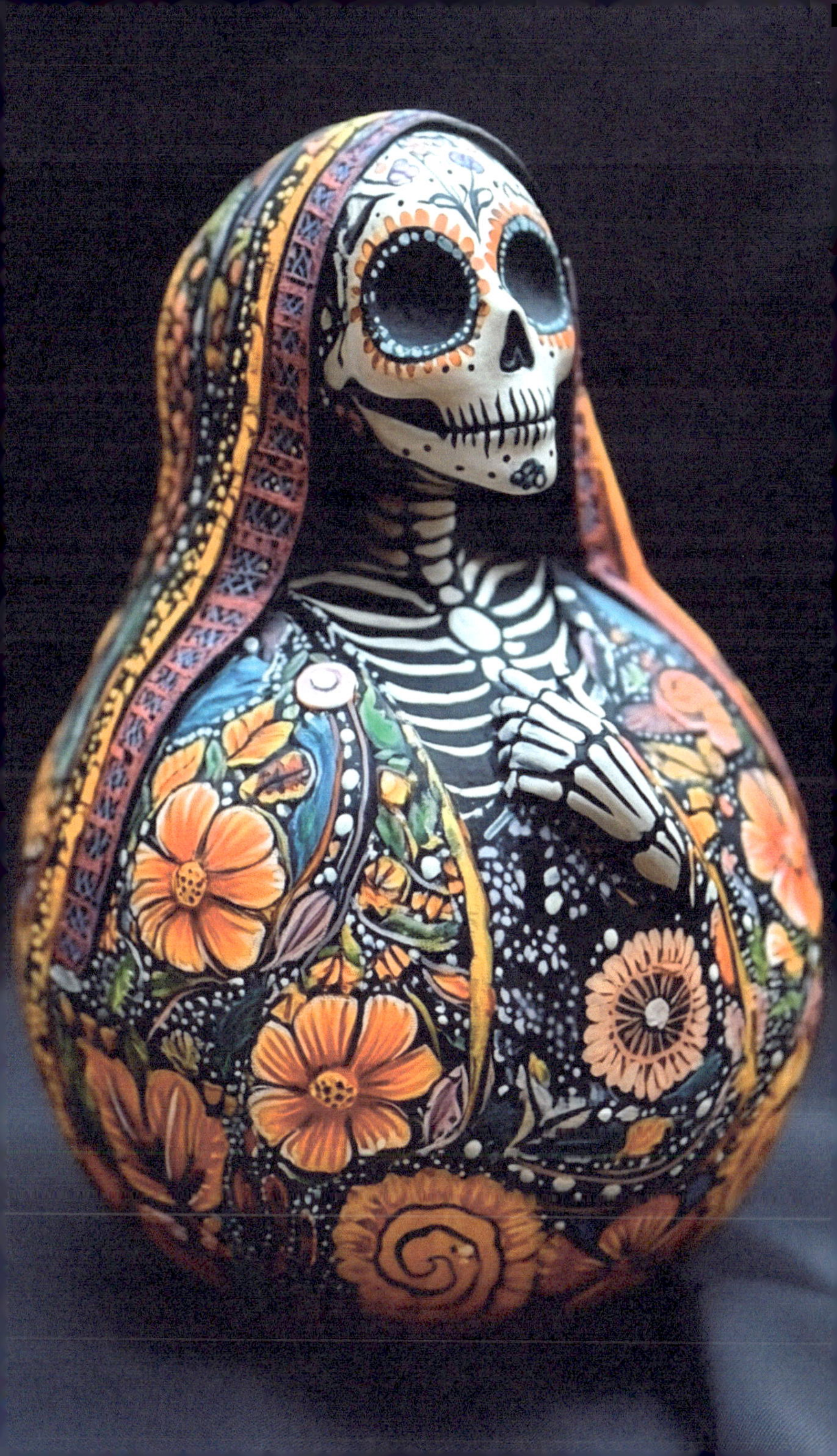

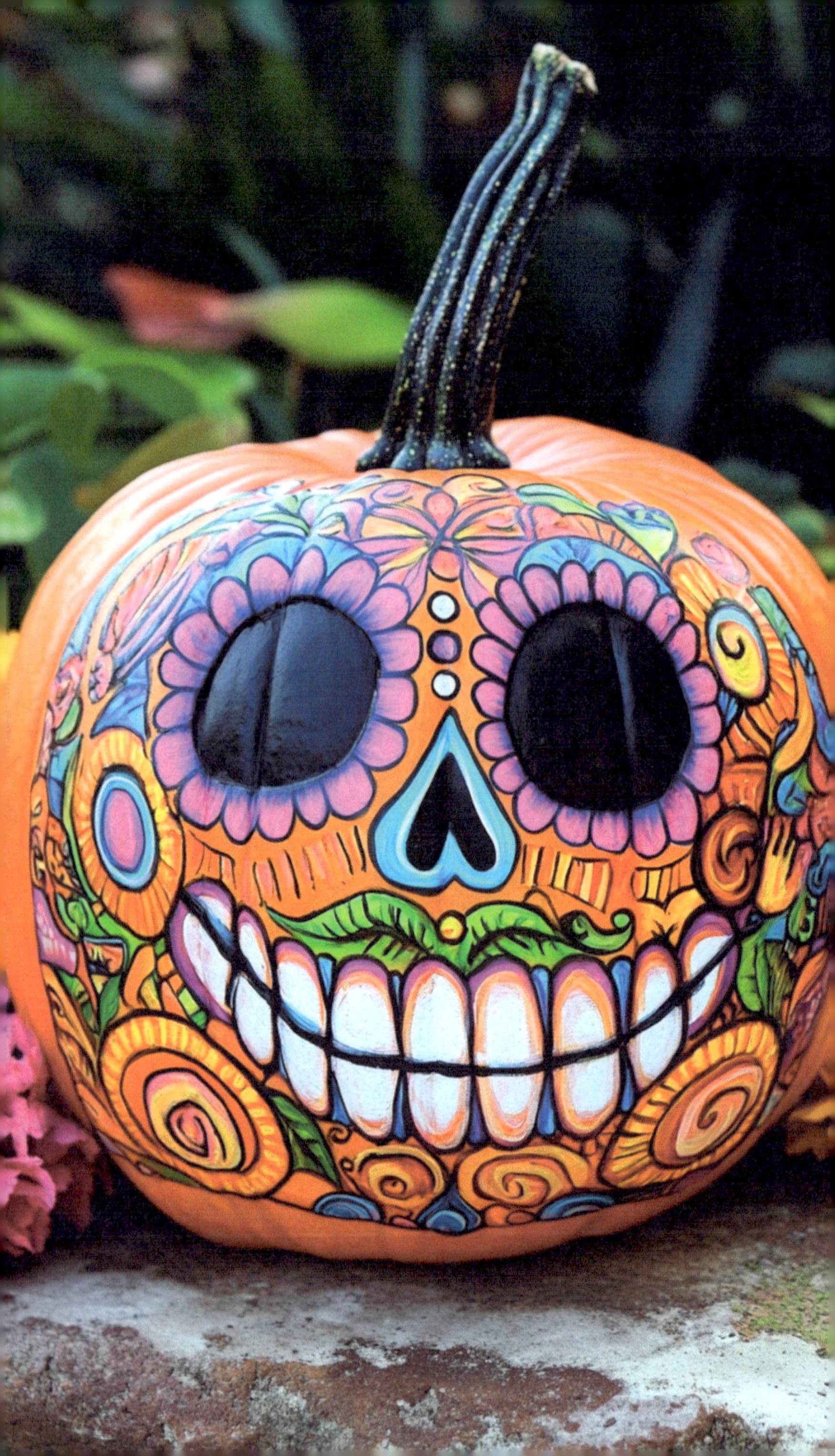

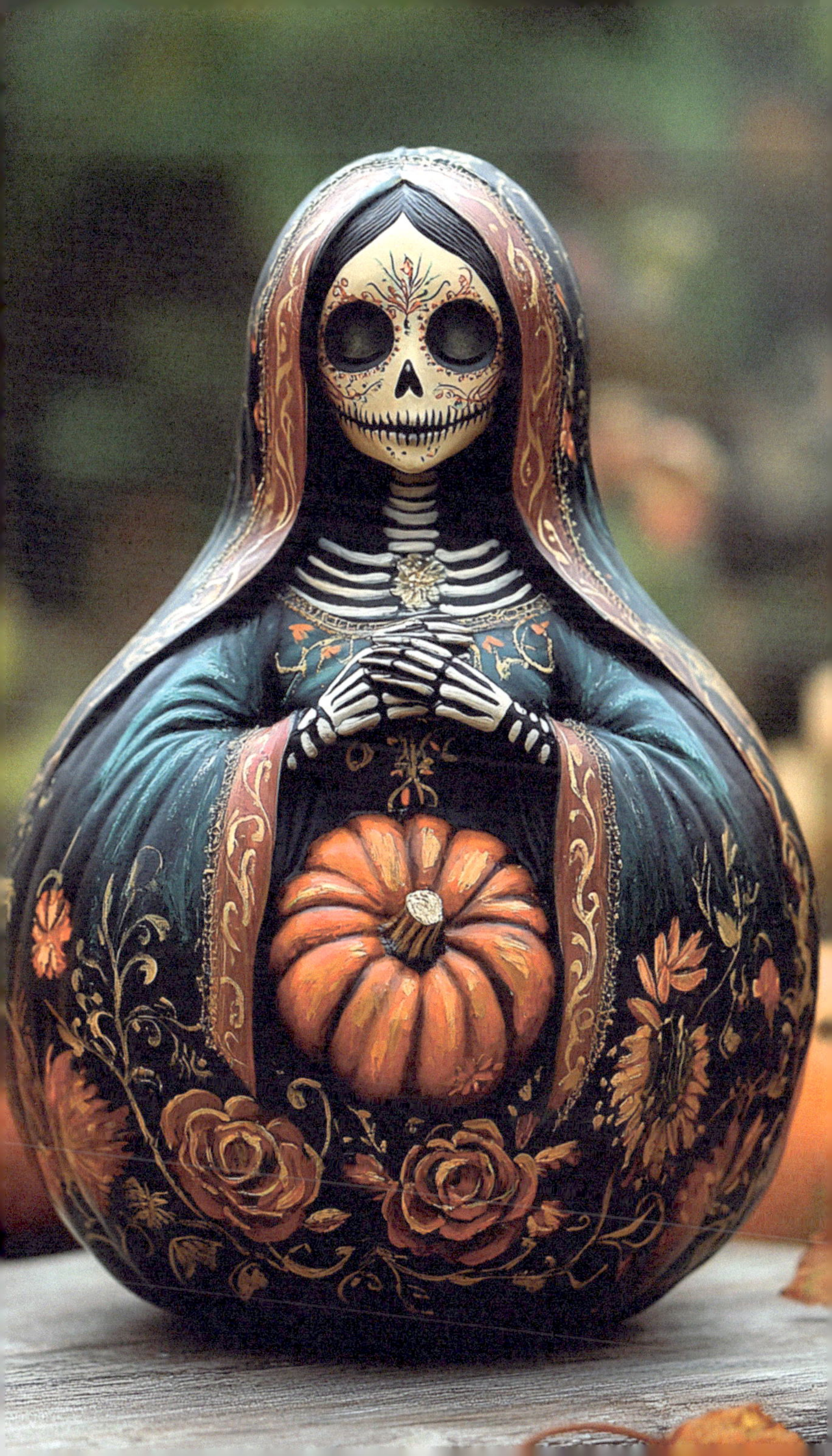

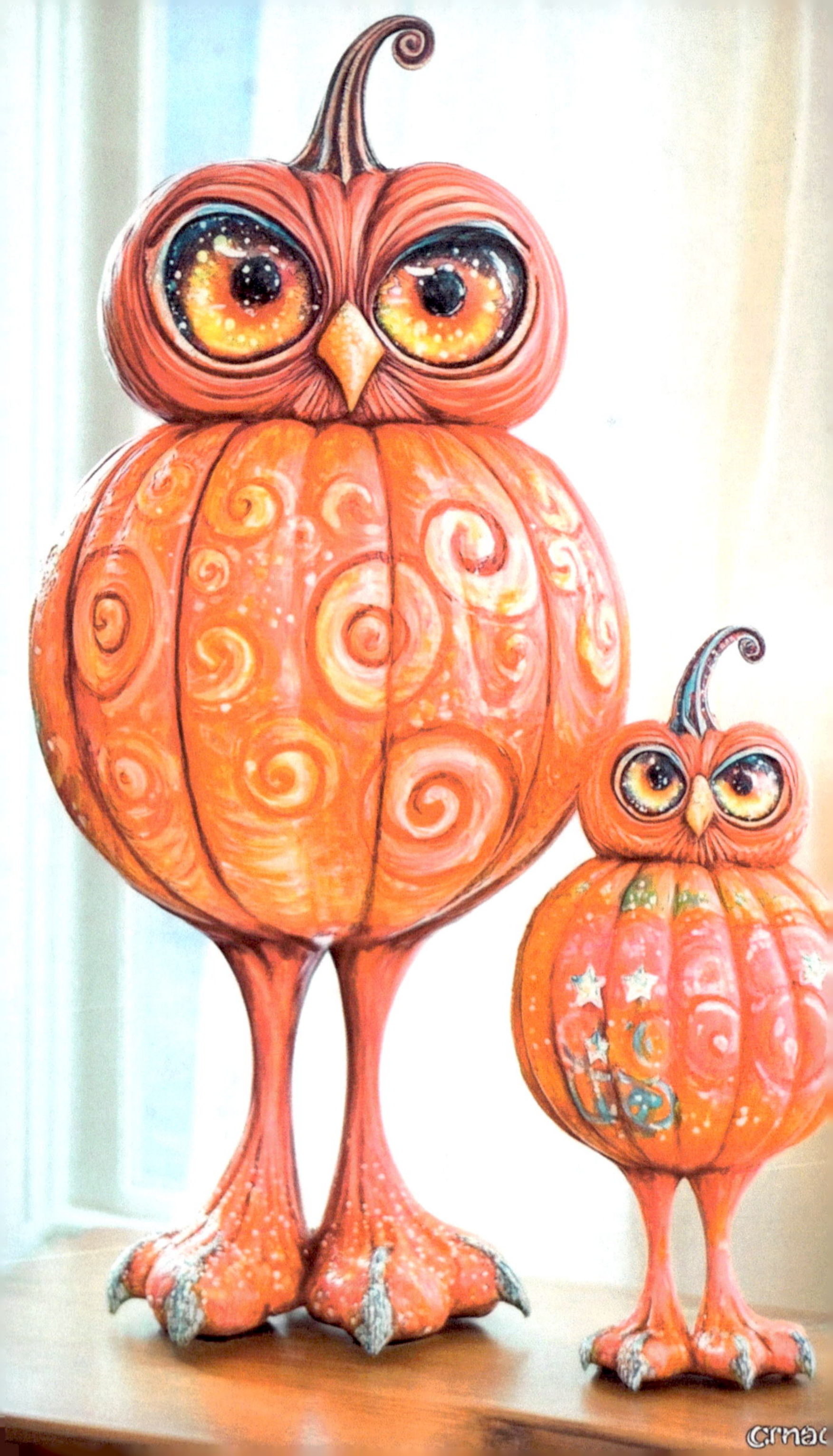

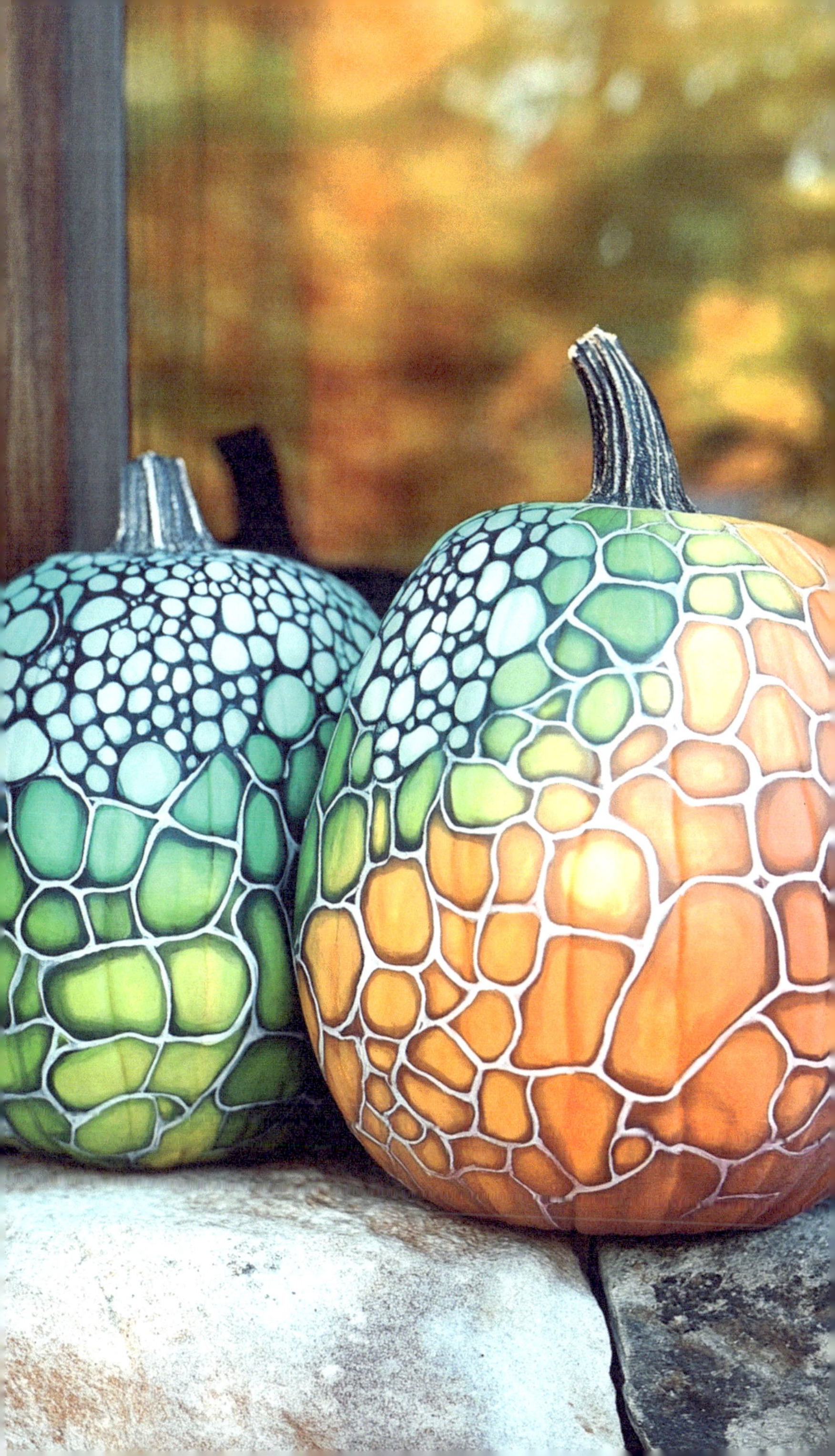

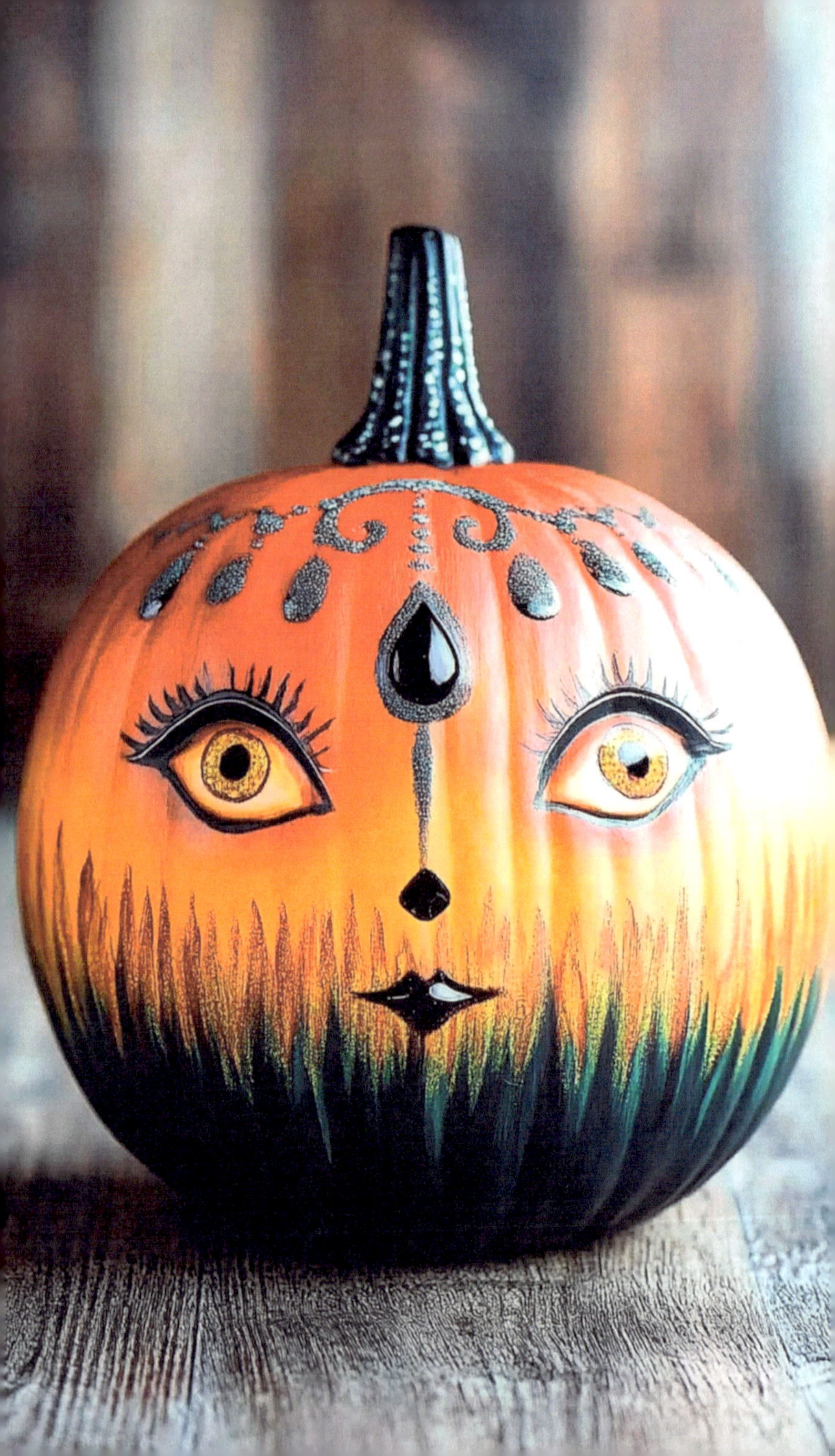

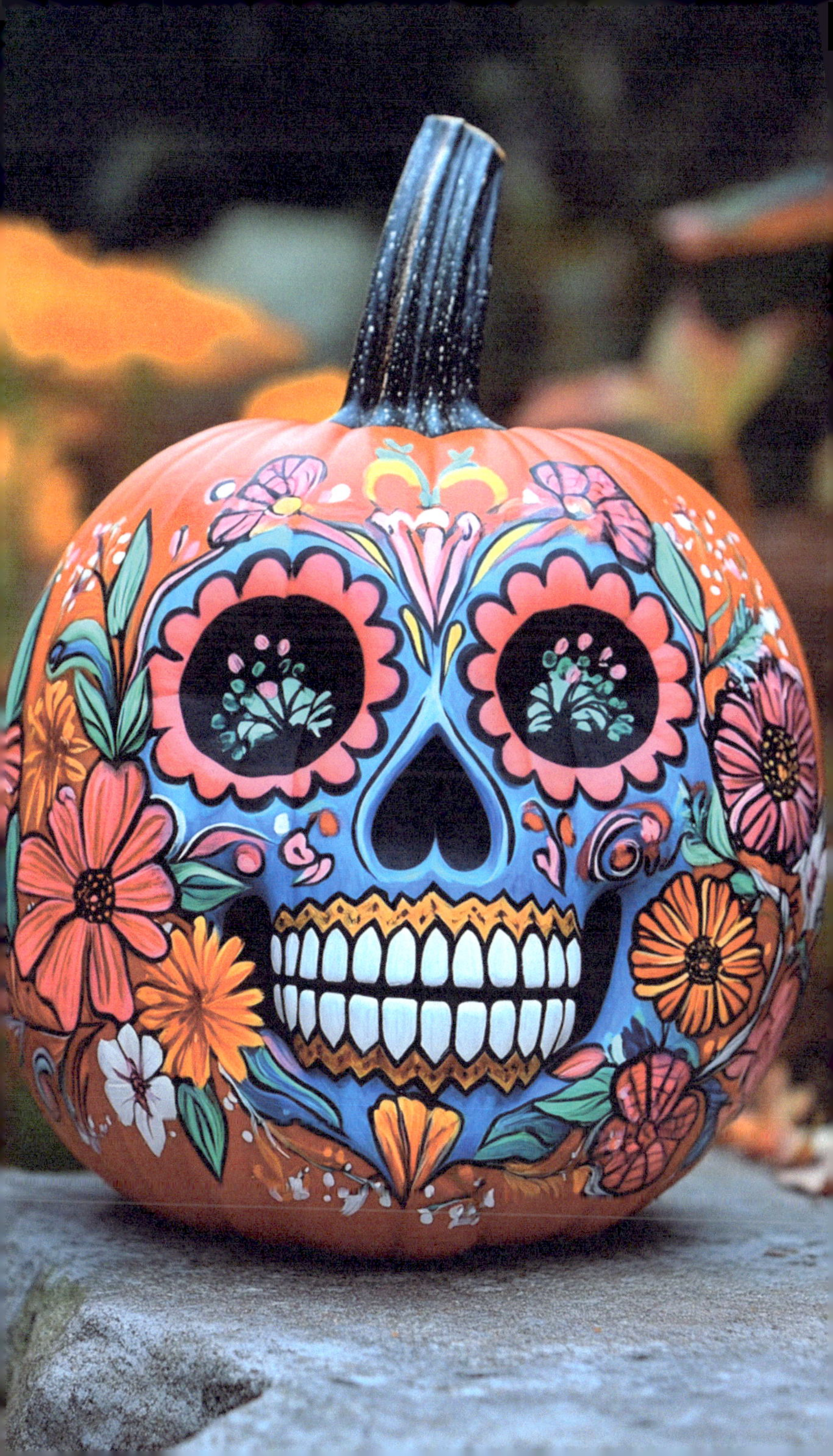

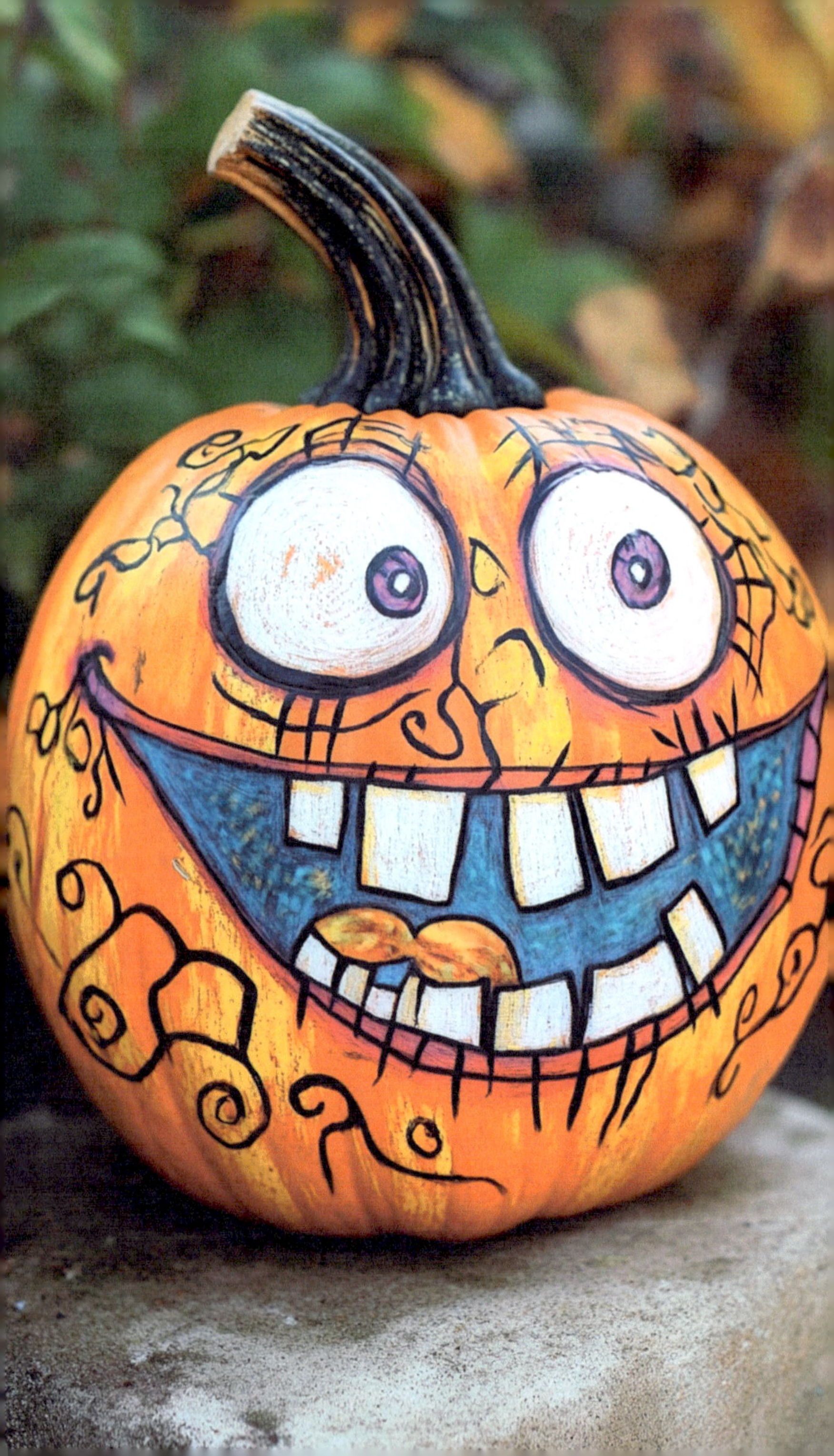

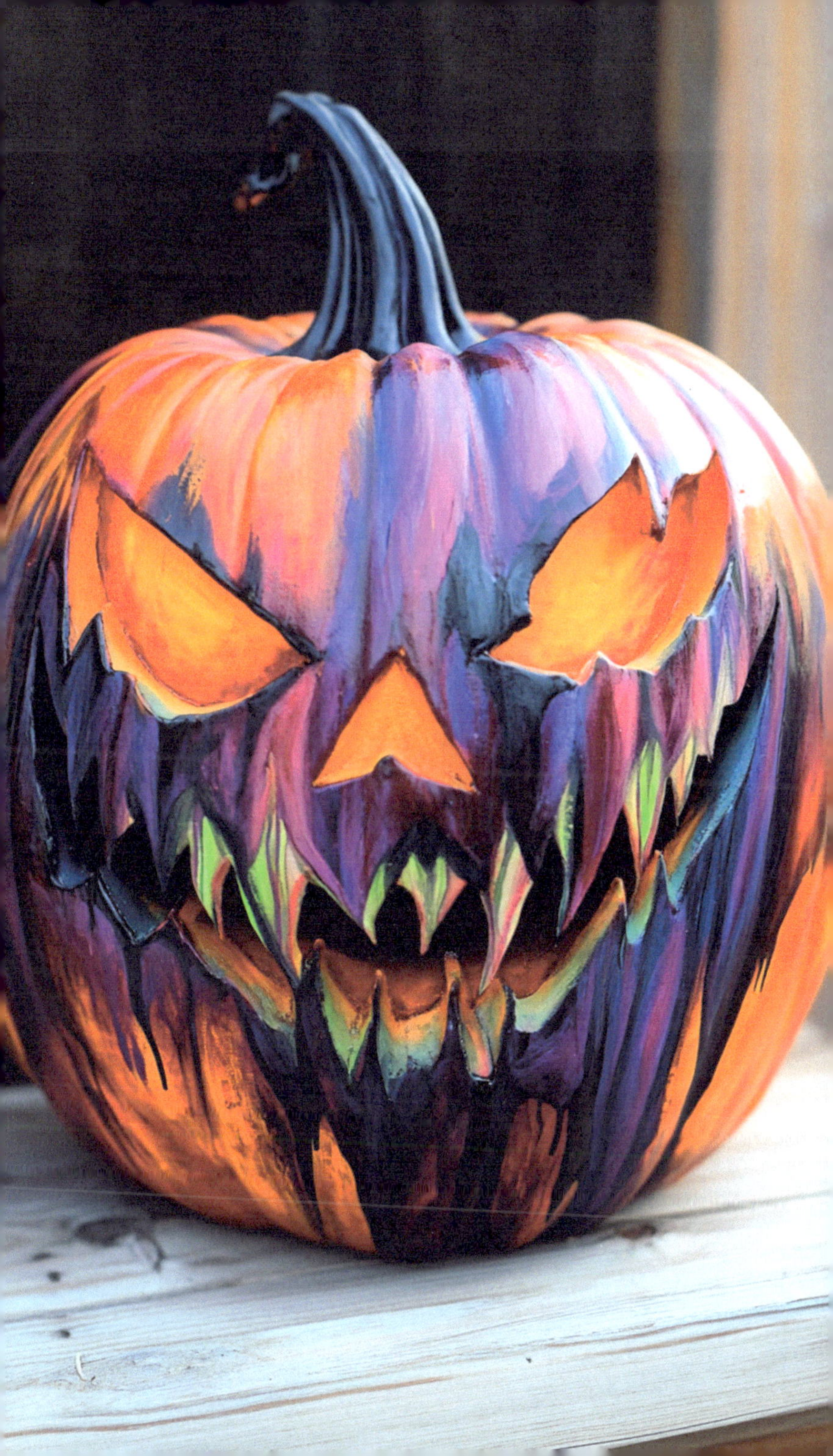

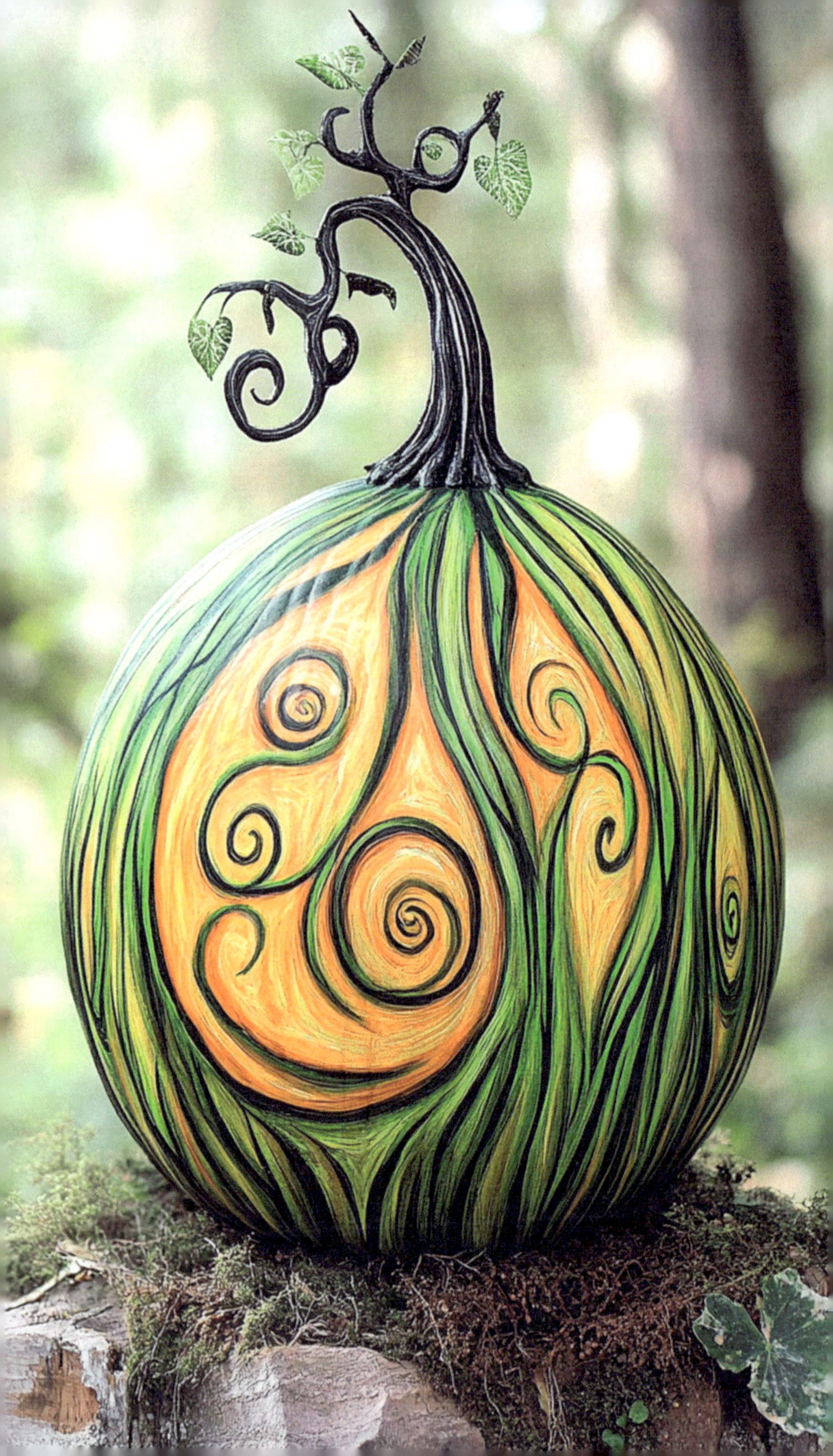

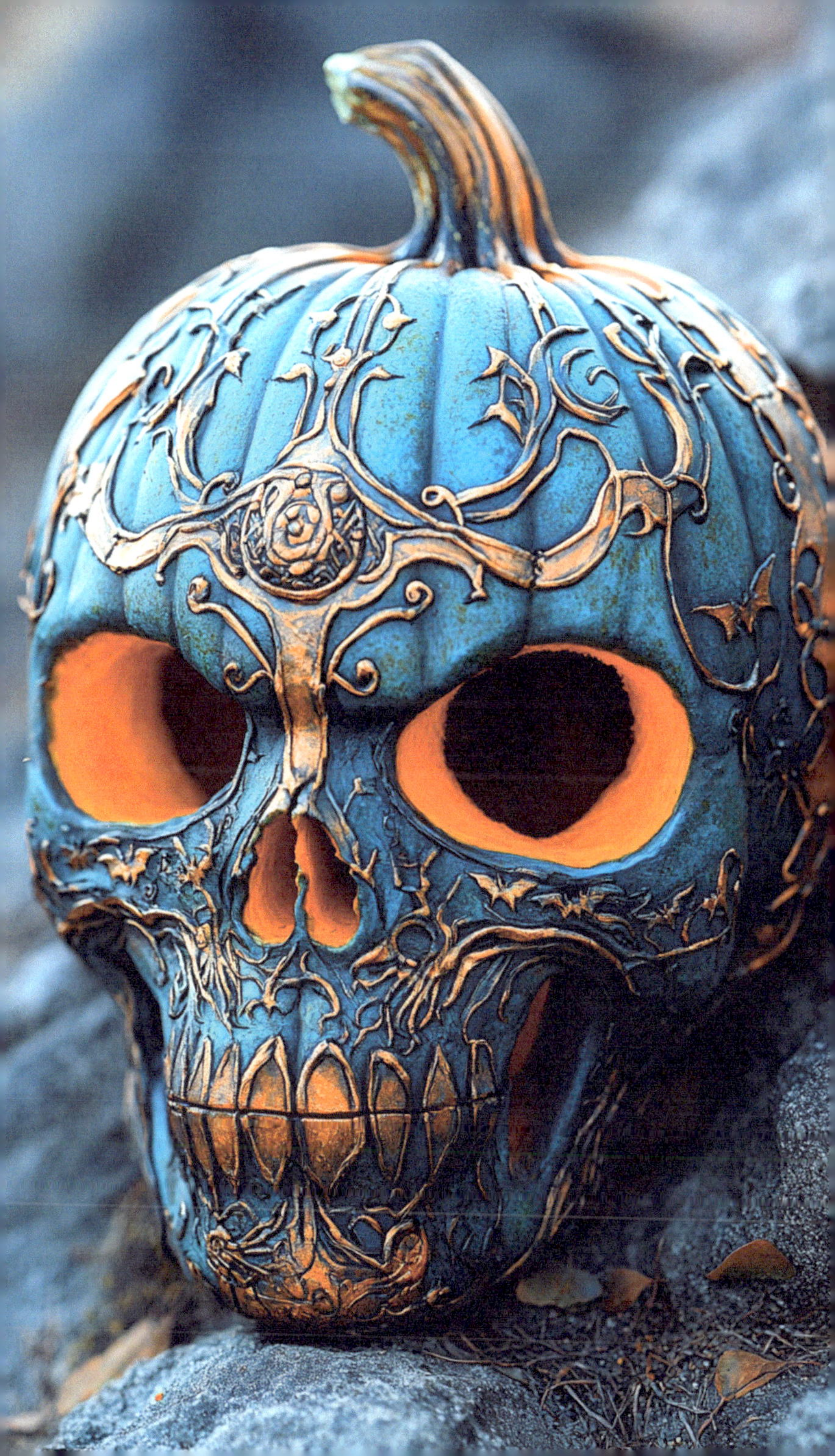

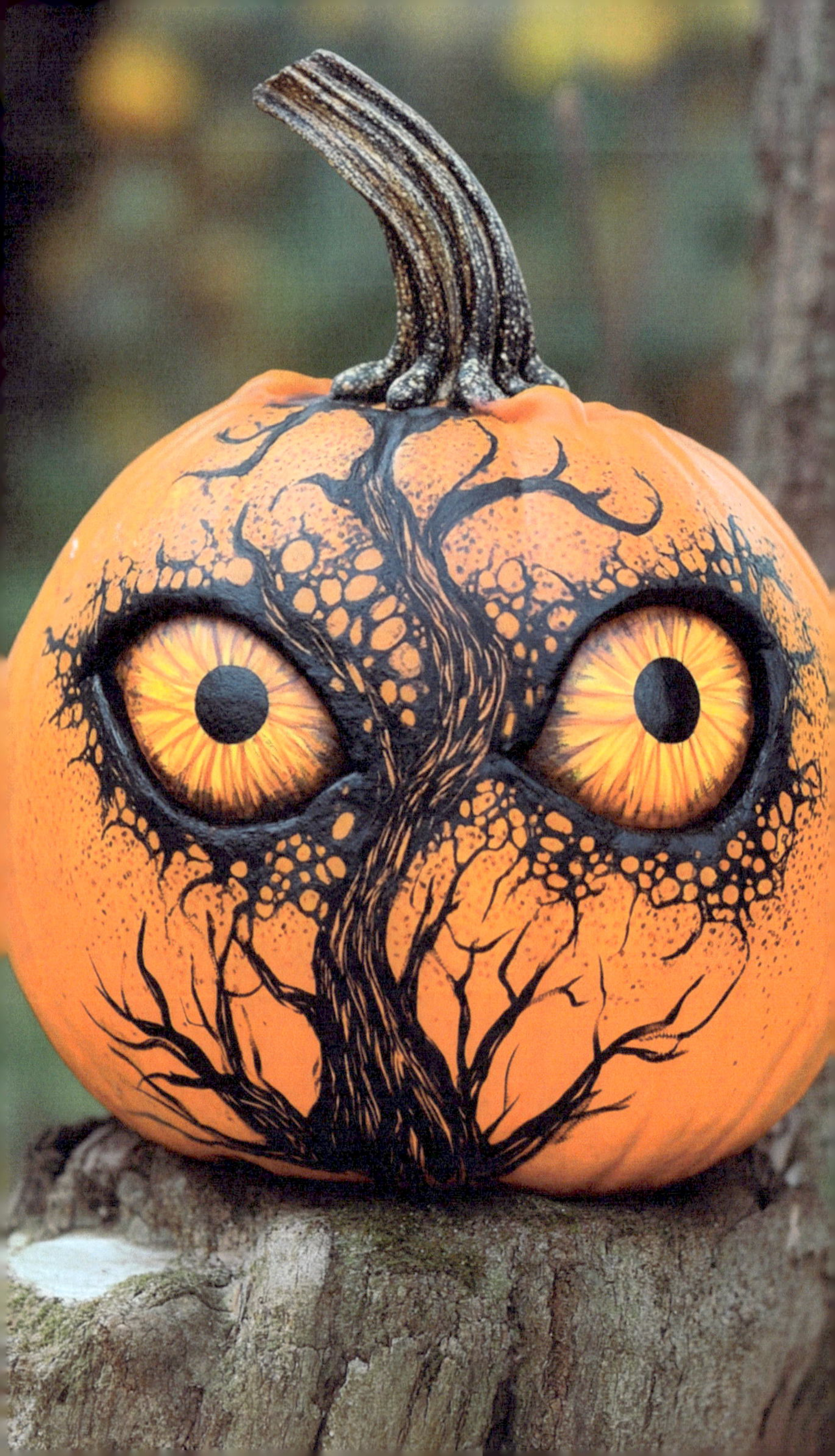

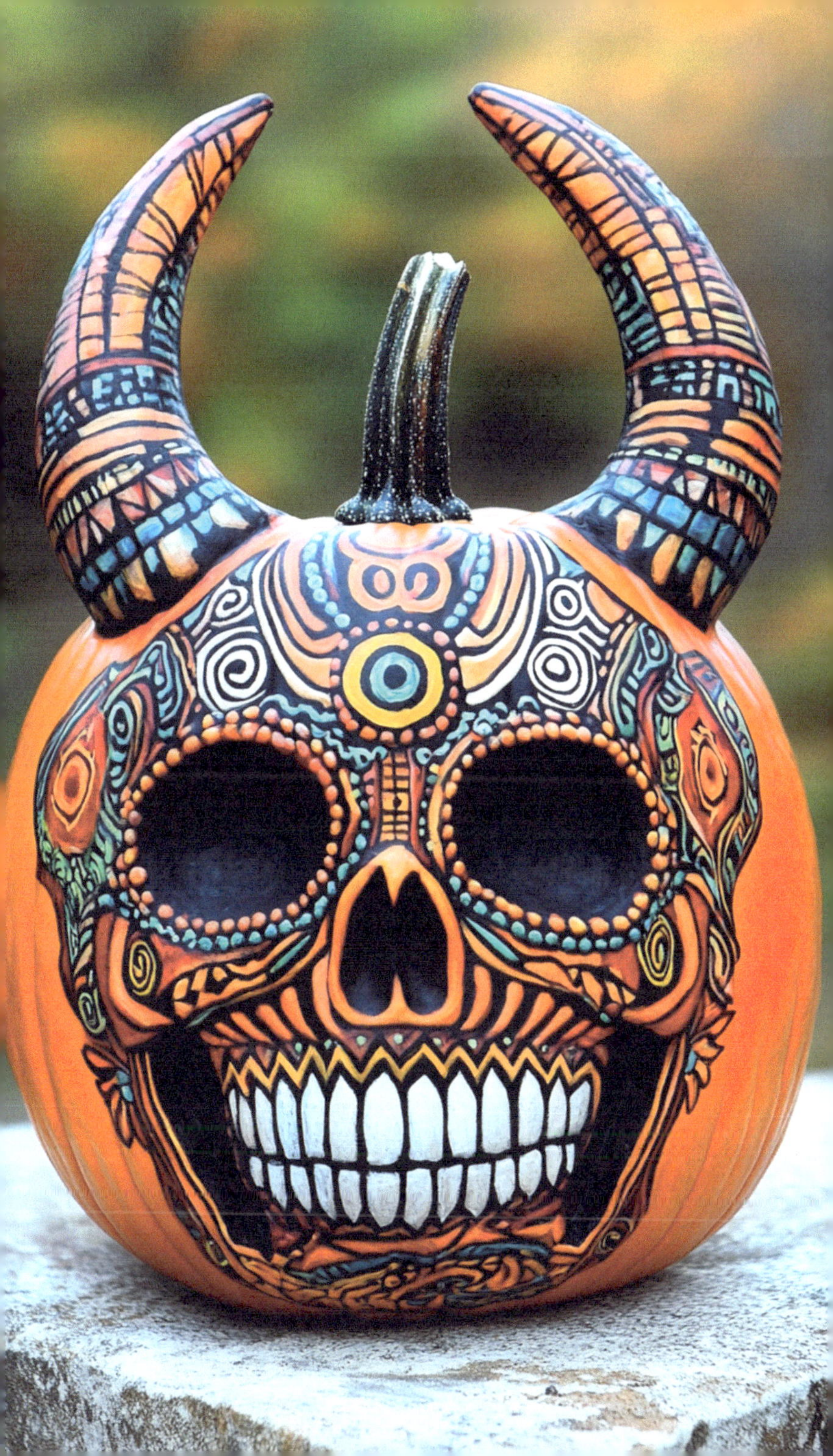

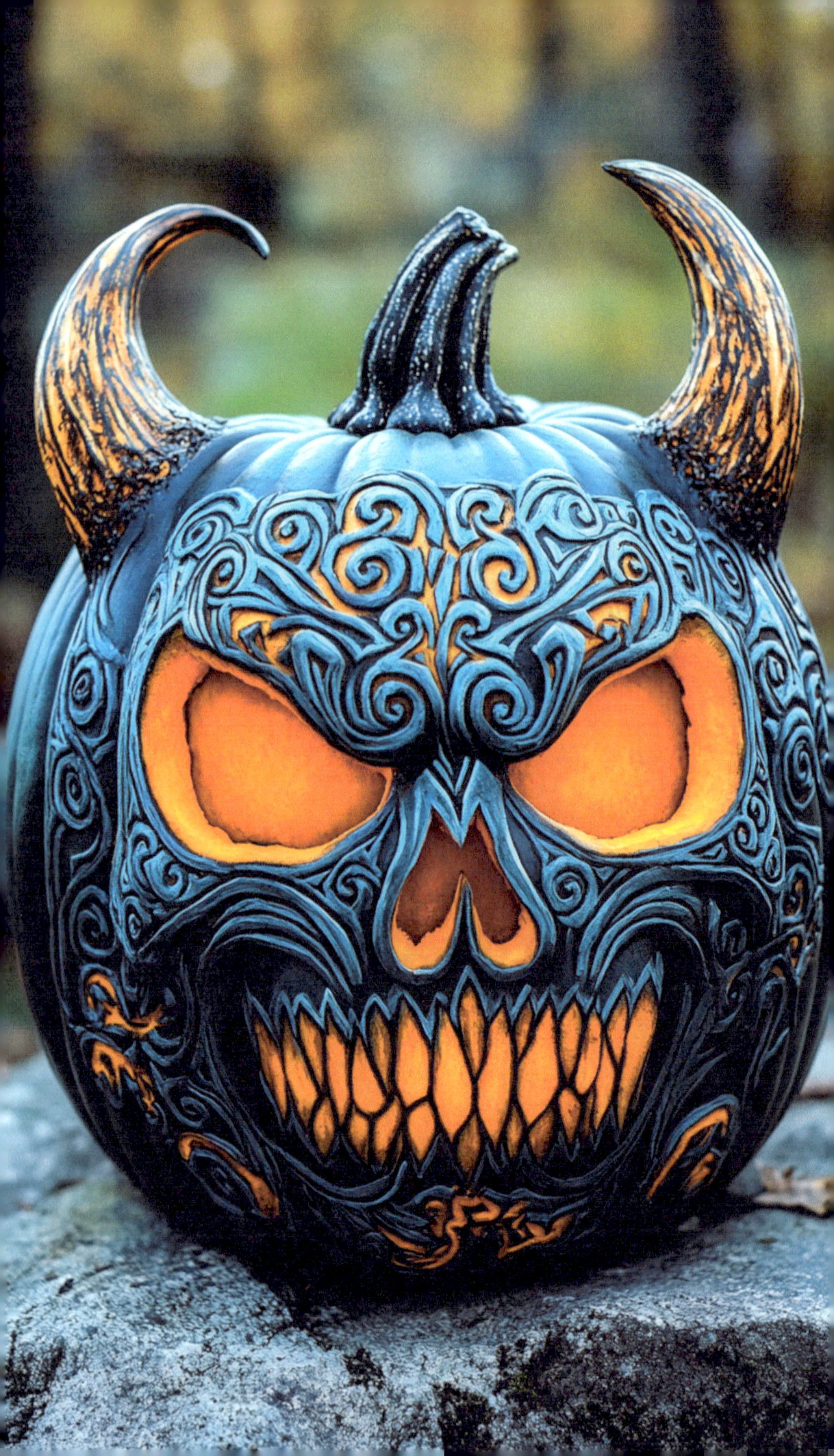

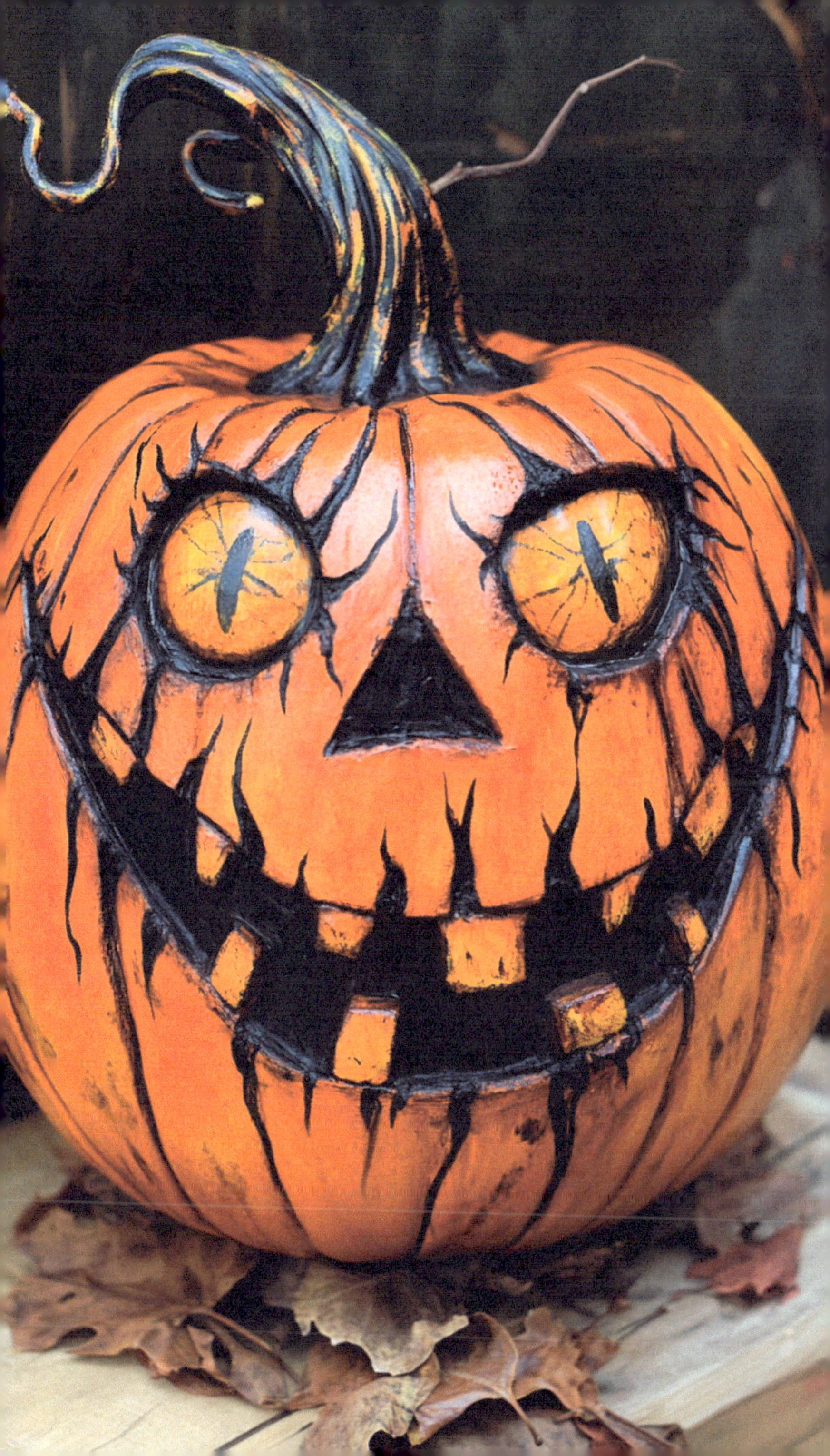

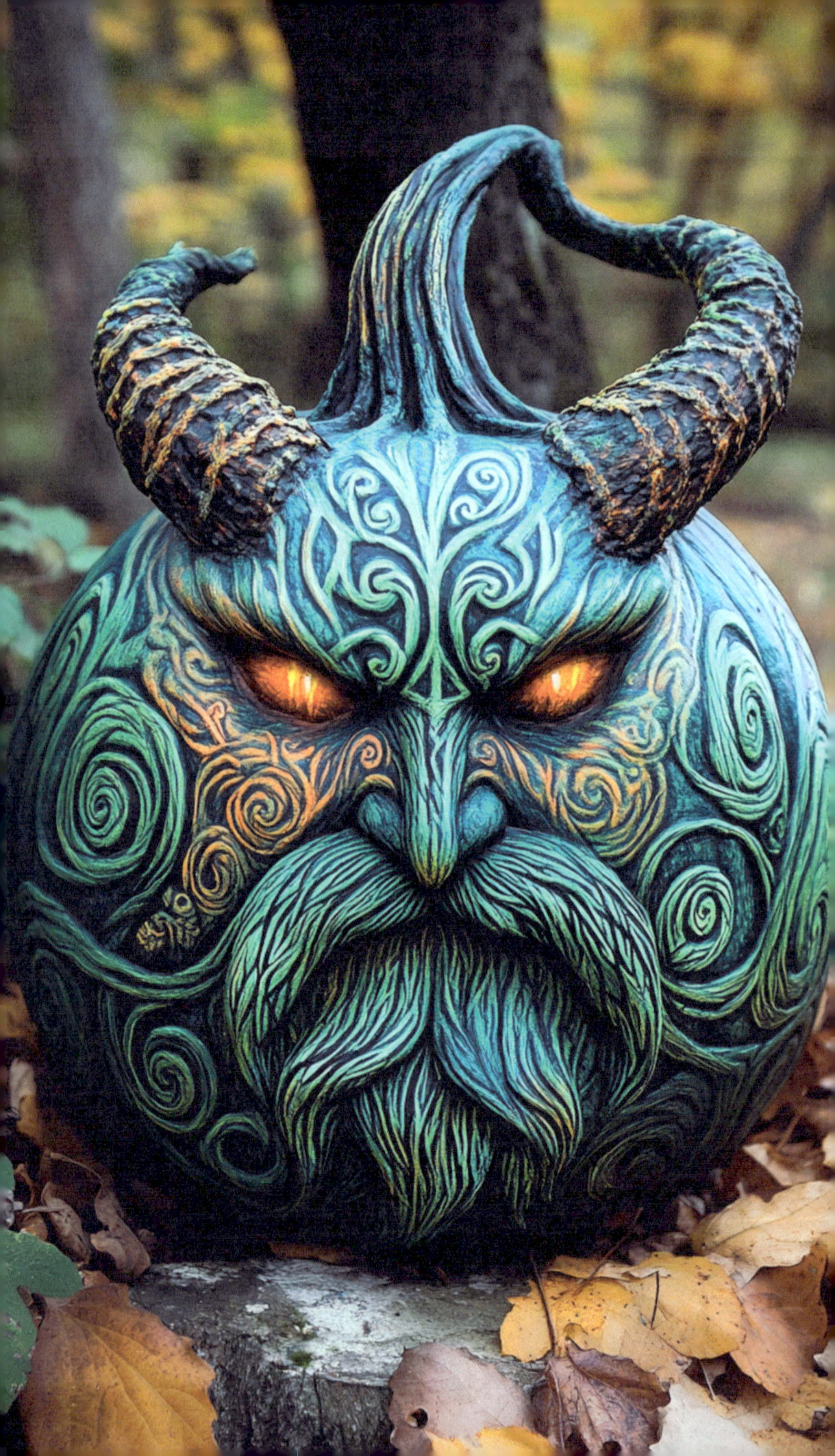

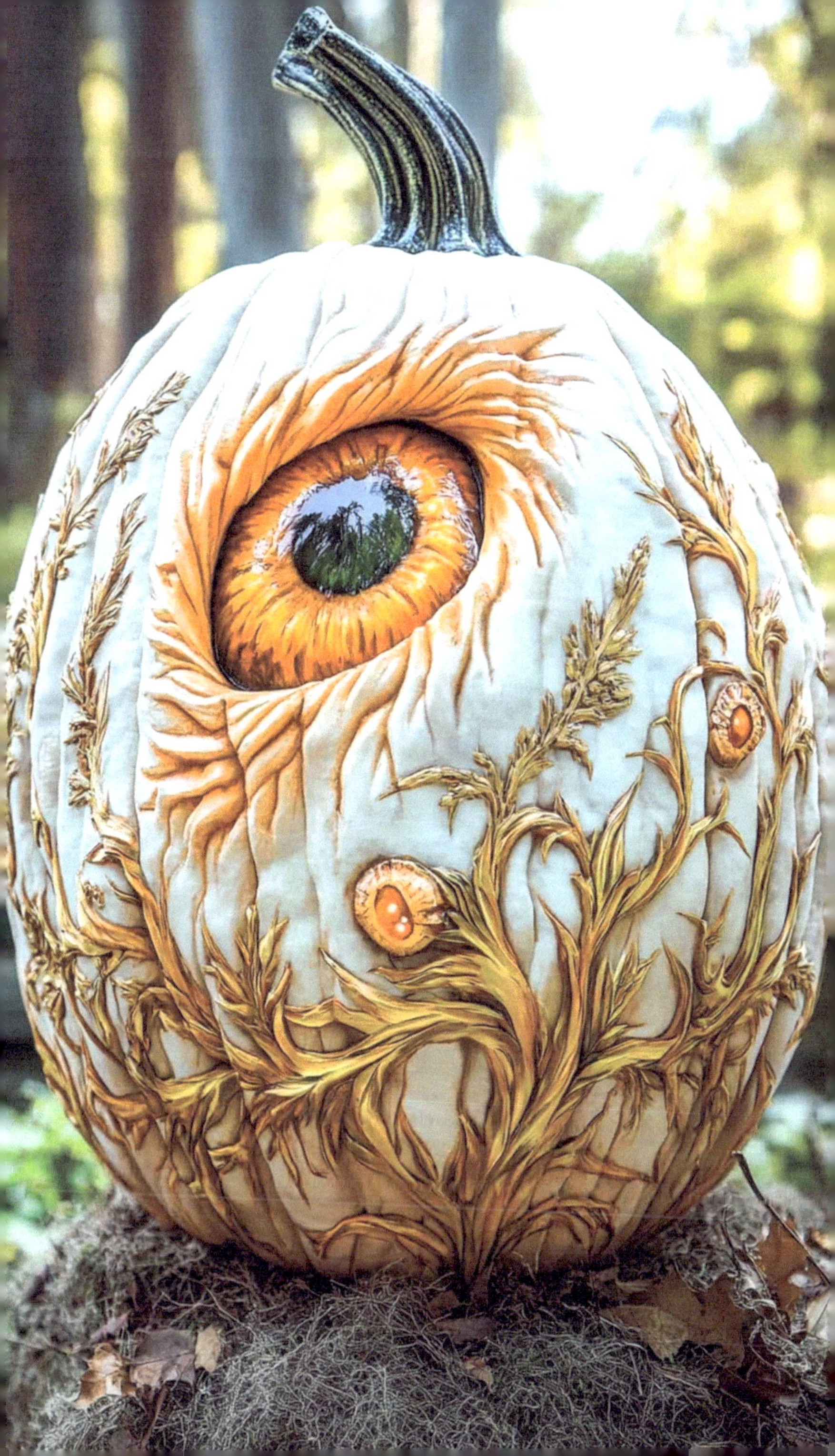

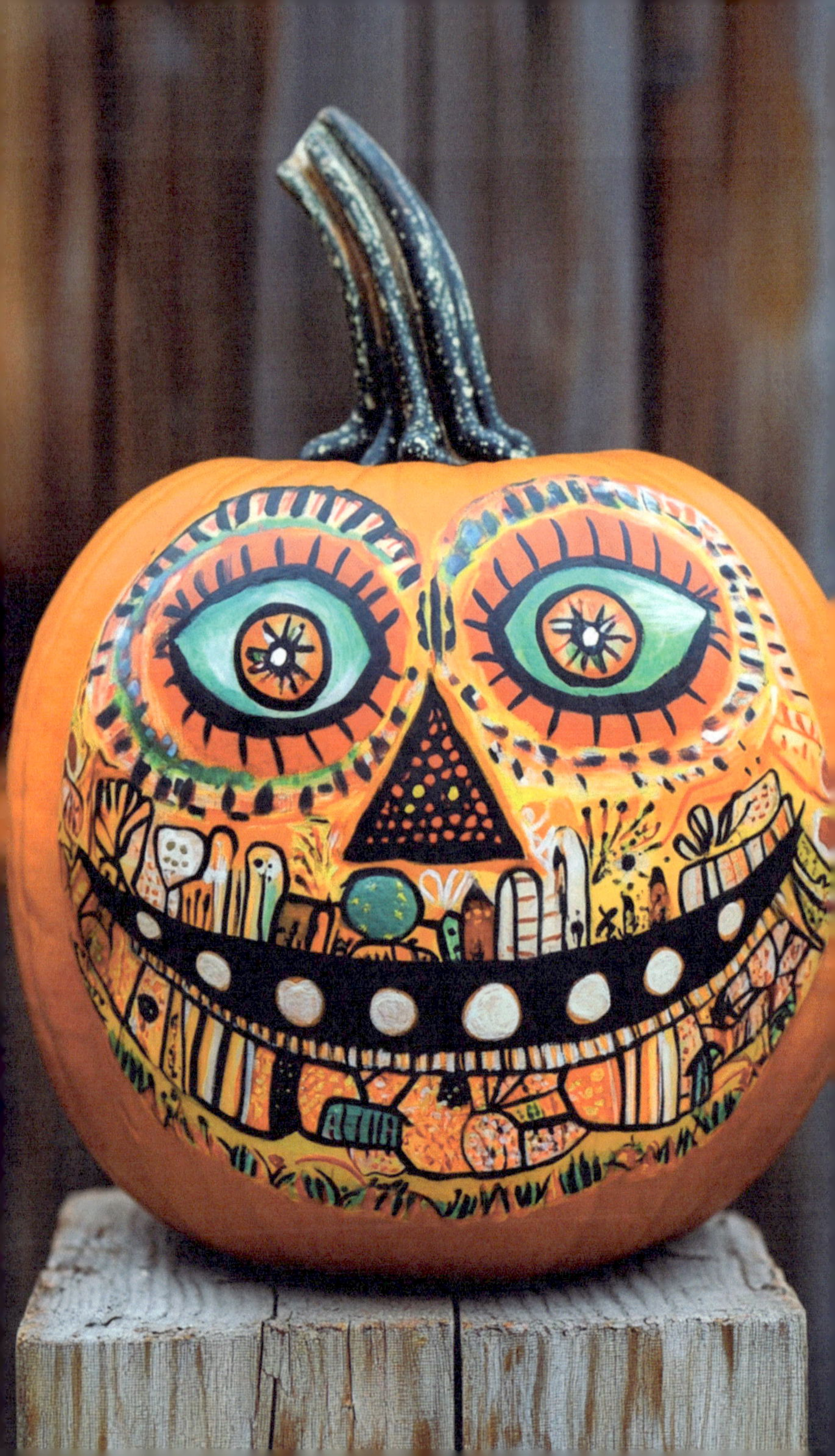

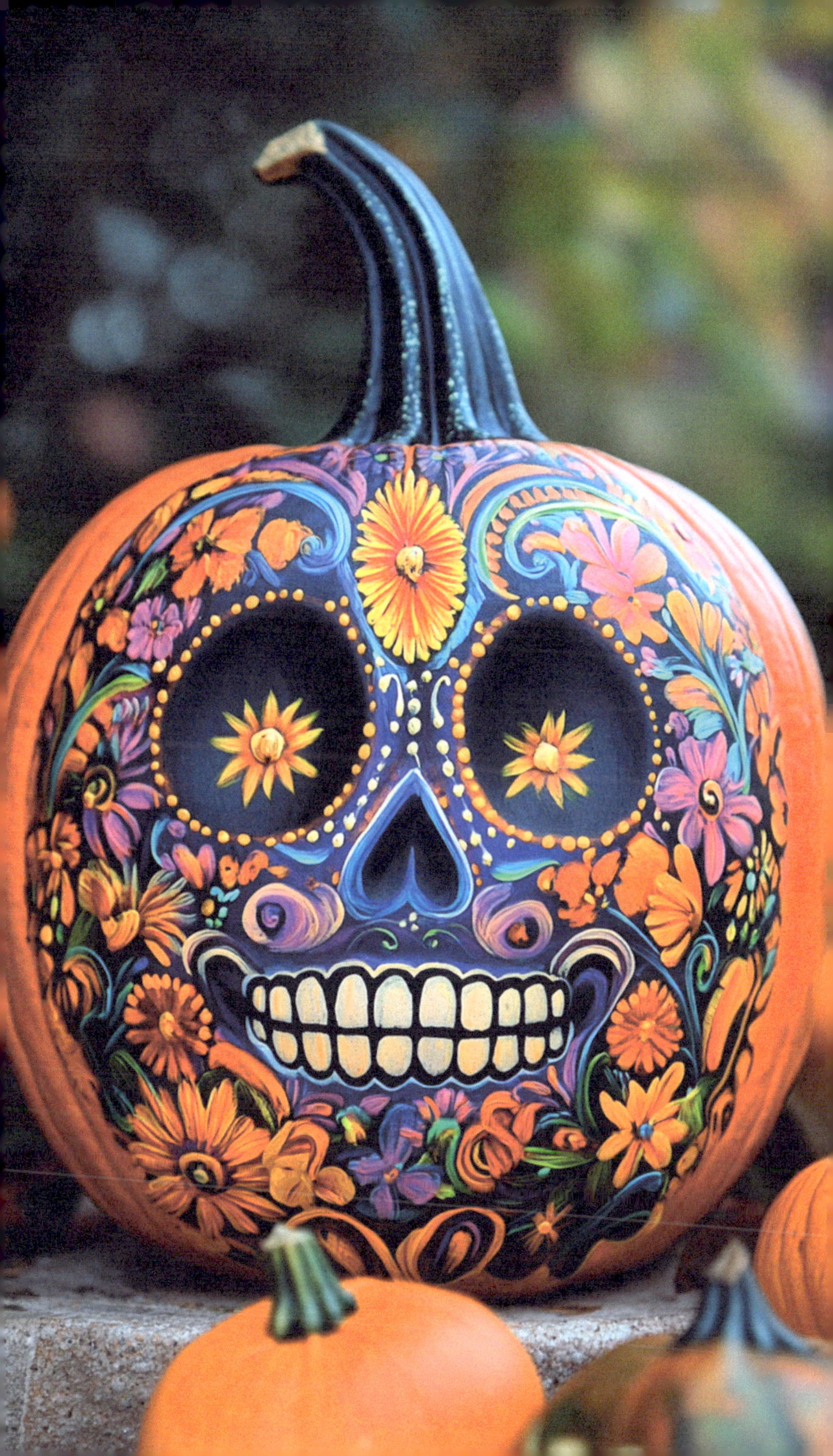

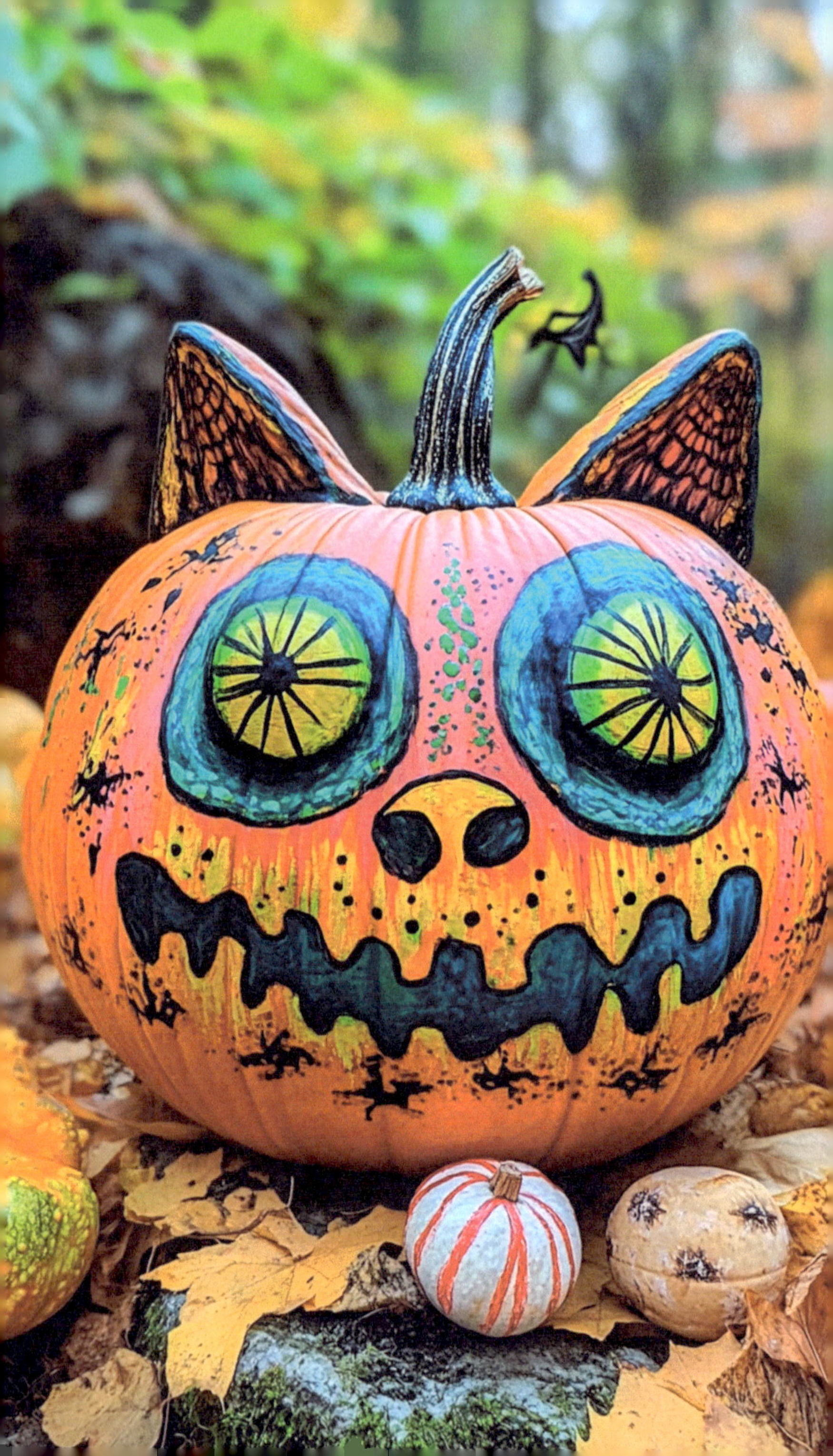

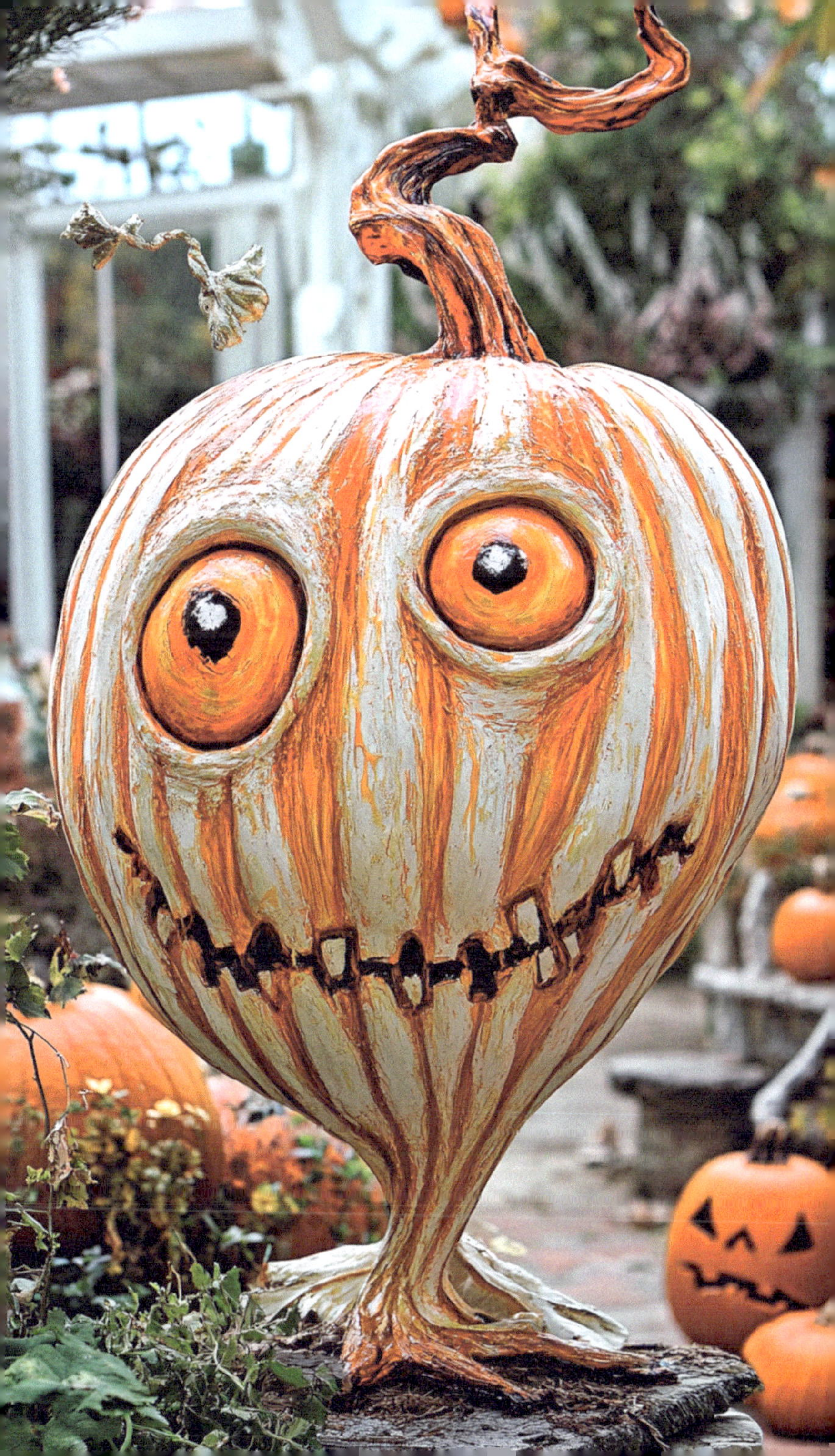

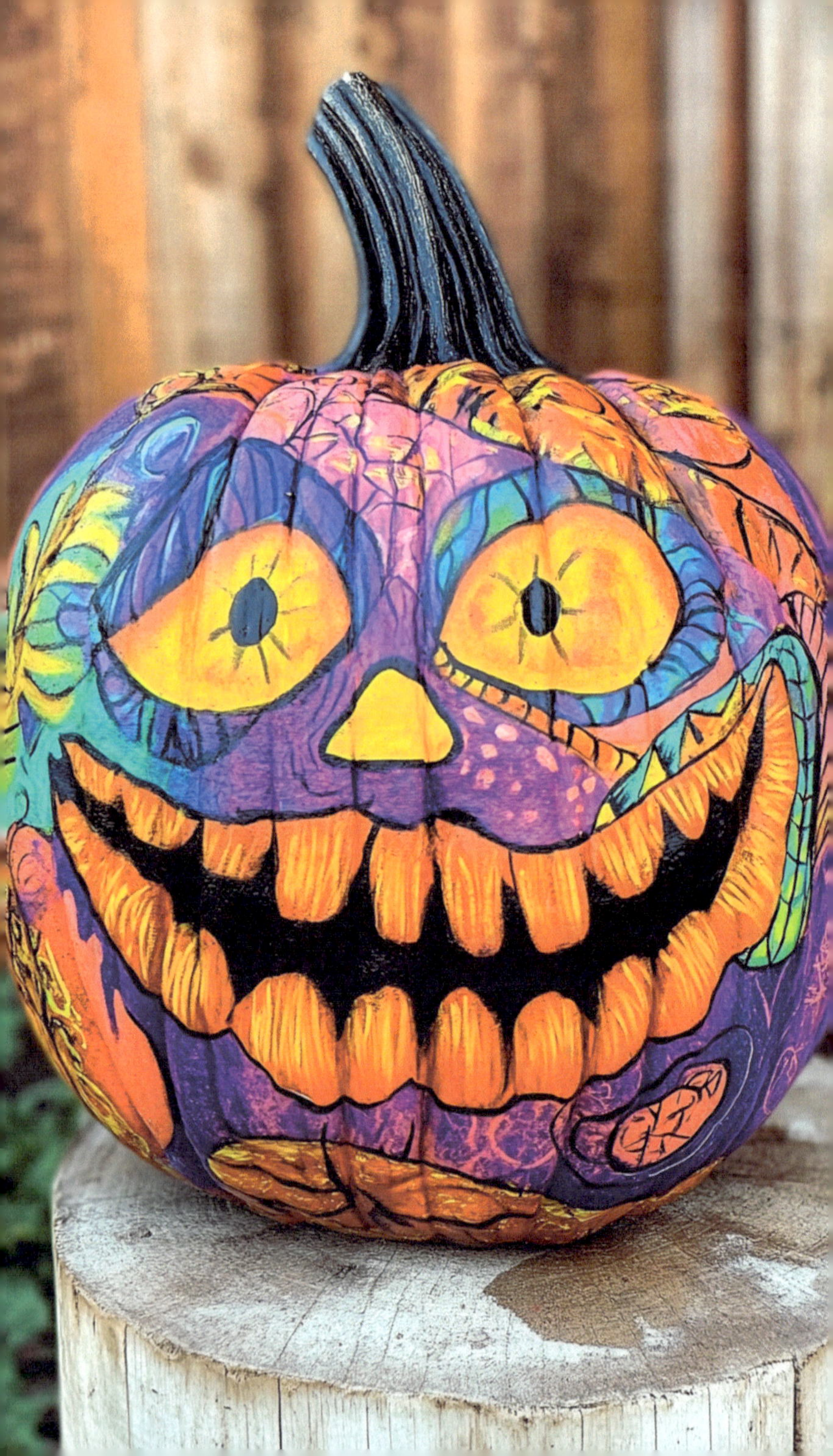

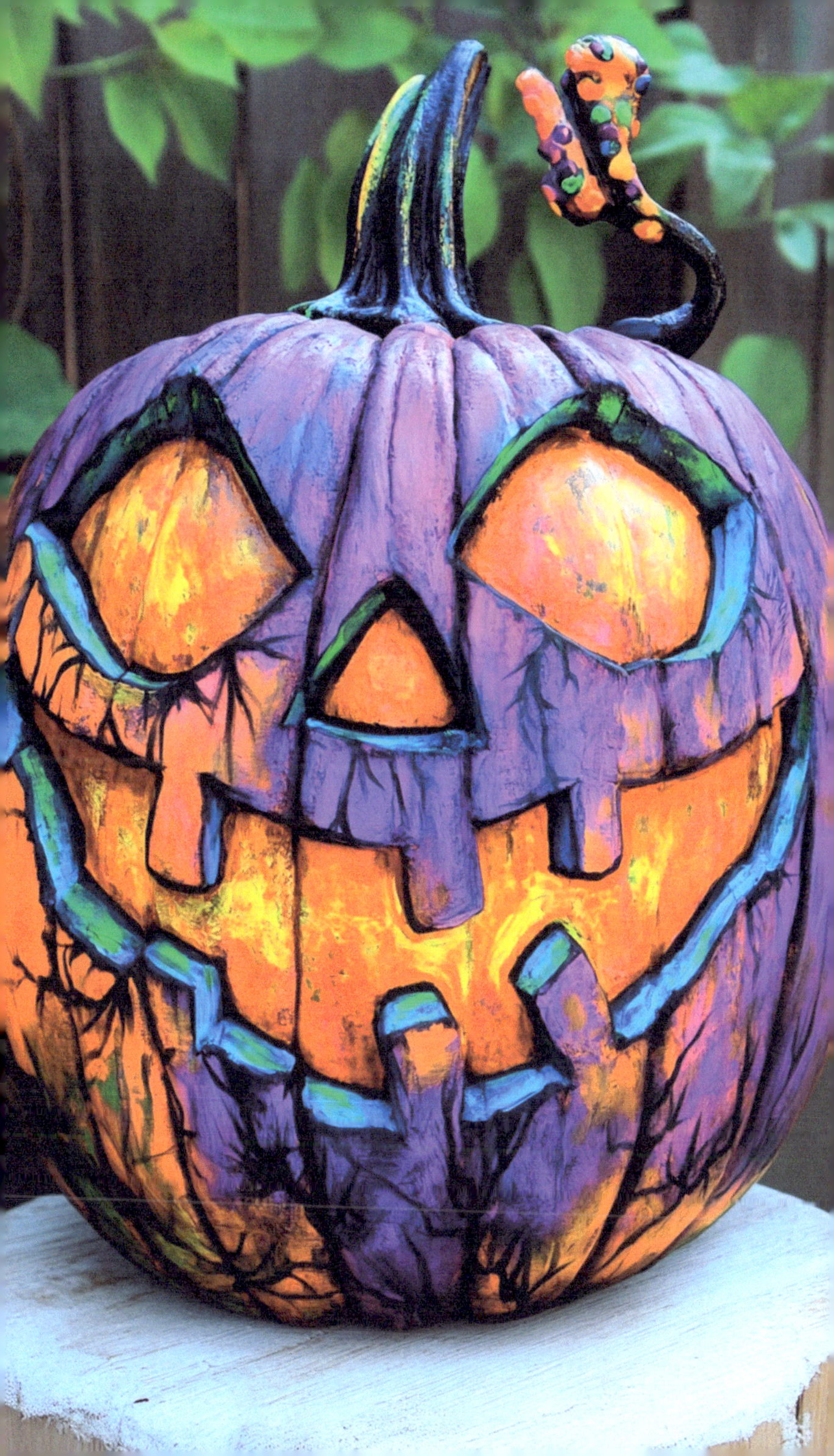

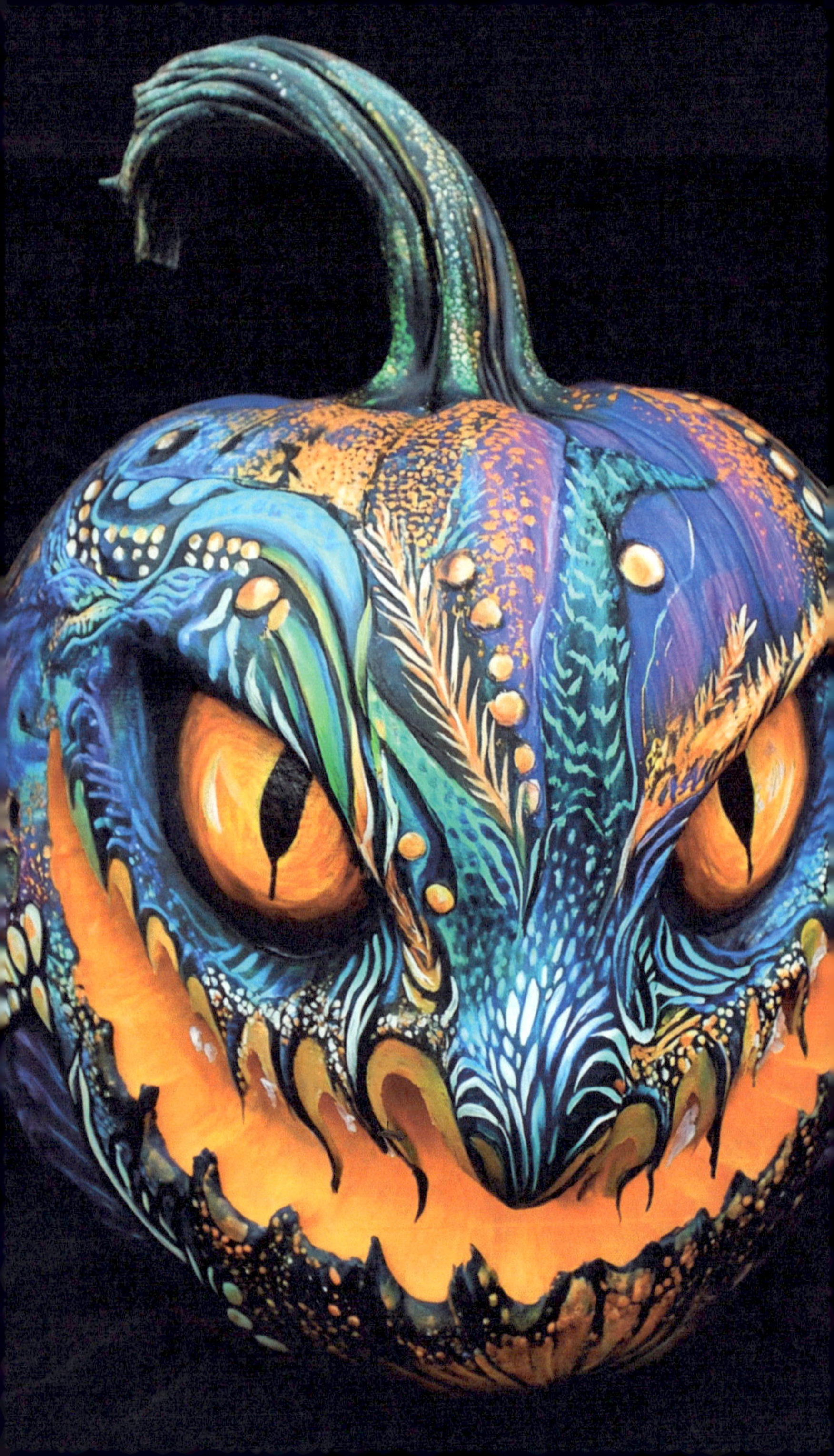

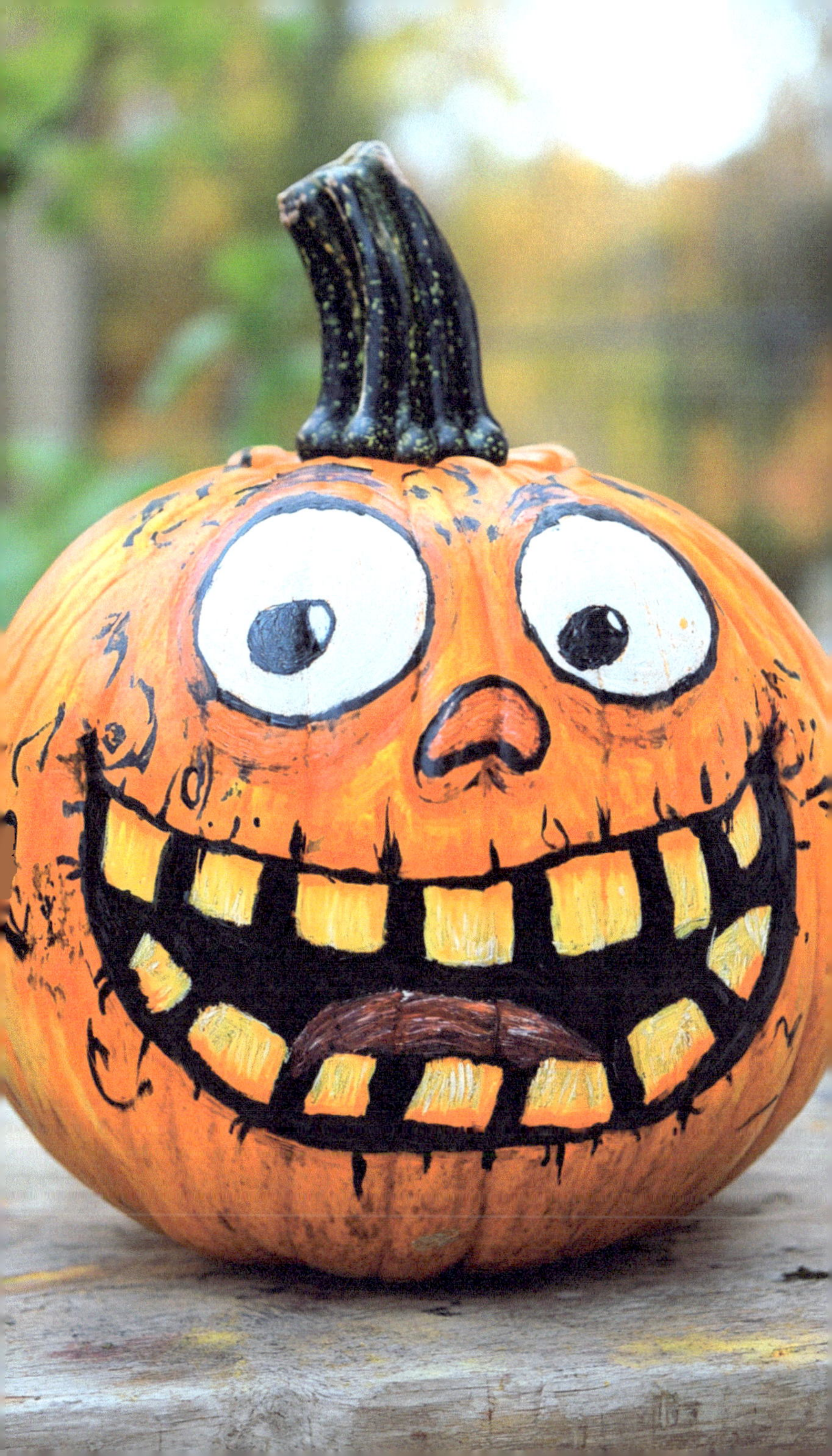

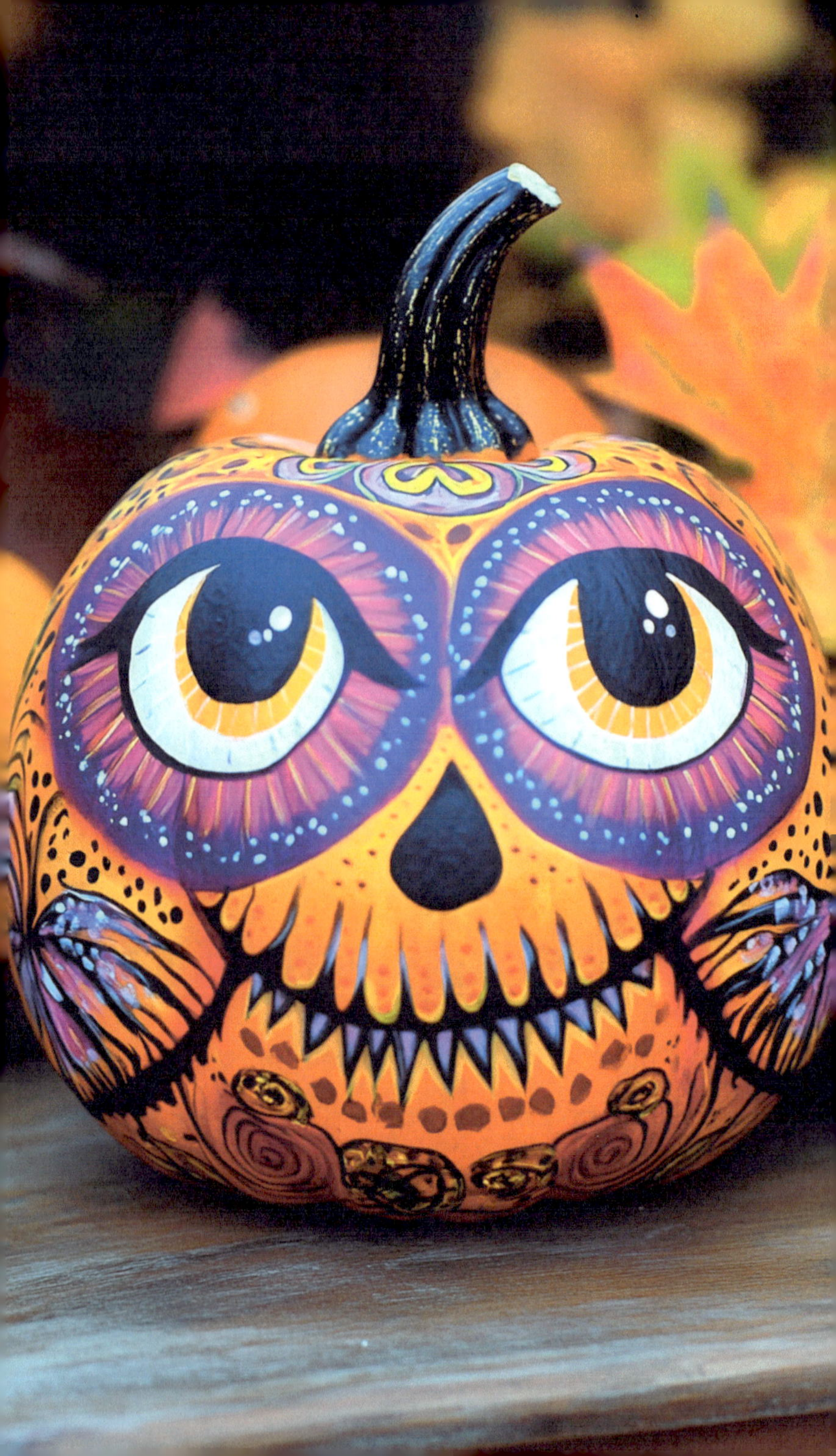

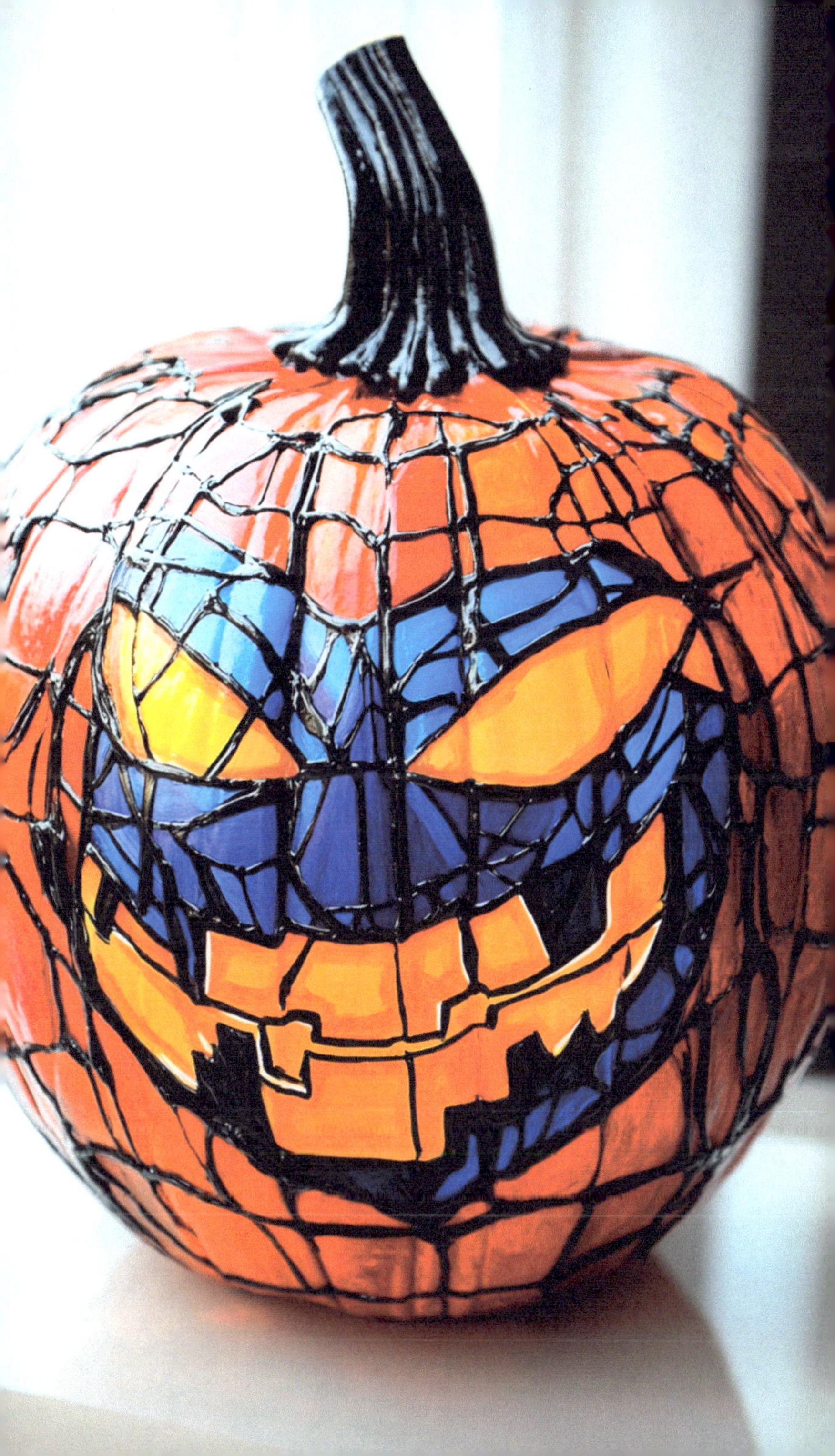

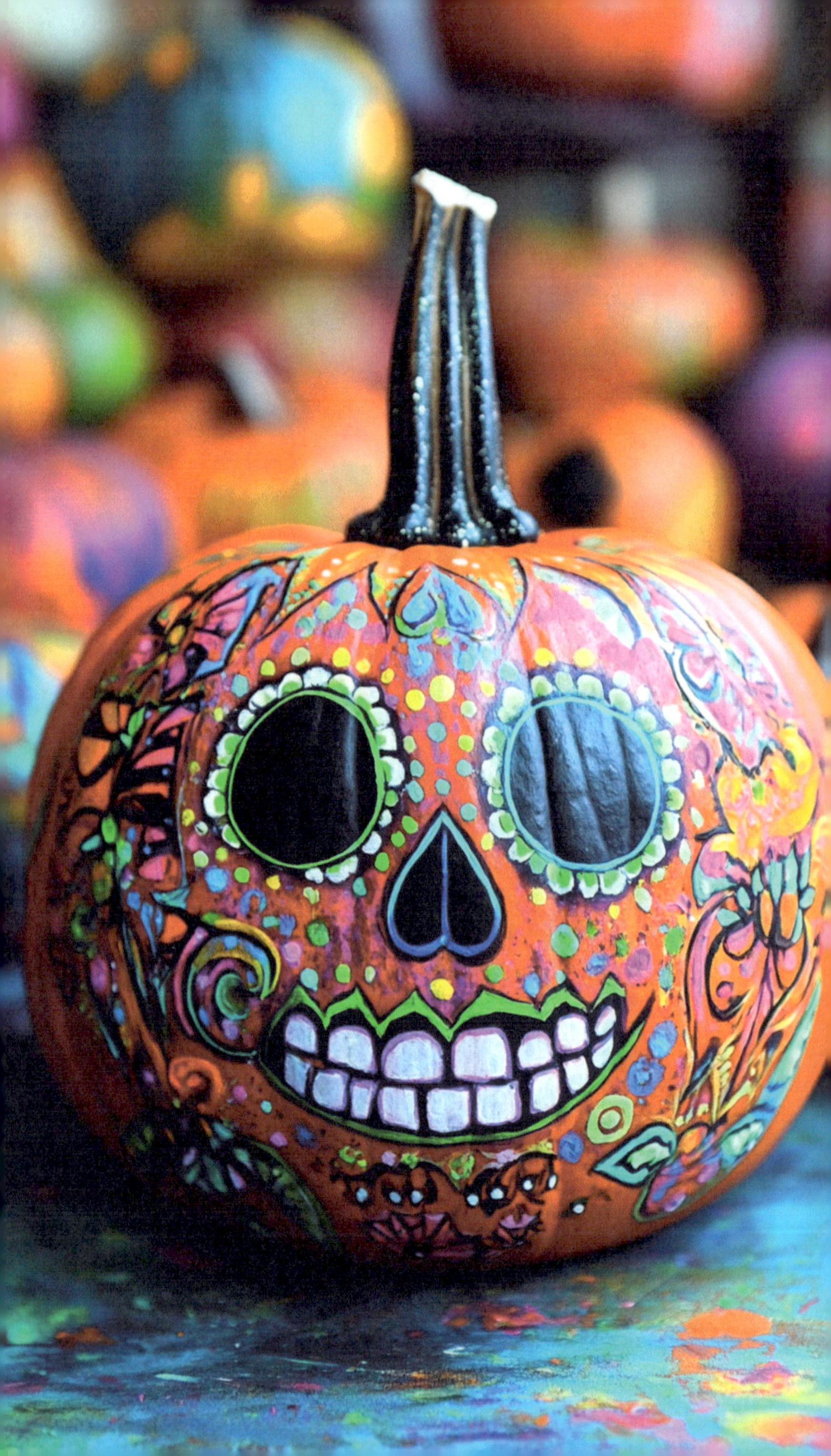

Made in the USA
Columbia, SC
26 October 2024